THE FIRST AMENDMENT

The ★★★★★★★ AMERICAN HERITAGE HISTORY *of the* BILL *of* RIGHTS

THE FIRST AMENDMENT

Philip A. Klinkner

Introduction by

WARREN E. BURGER

Chief Justice of the United States
1969–1986

Silver Burdett Press

To Marie and her generation. May they protect and expand the rights and liberties of all Americans.

Cover: Demonstrators exercise their First Amendment rights of freedom of speech and freedom of assembly near the Capitol building, Washington, D.C.

CONSULTANTS:

Maria Cedeño
Social Studies Coordinator,
 Region 4
Law-Related Education
 Coordinator
Dade County Public Schools
Miami, Florida

Richard M. Haynes
Assistant Professor
Division of Administration,
 Instruction, and Curriculum
Western Carolina University
Cullowhee, North Carolina

Herbert Sloan
Assistant Professor of History
Barnard College
New York, New York

Text and Cover Design: Circa 86, Inc.

Copyright © 1991 by Gallin House Press, Inc.
Introduction copyright © 1991 by Silver Burdett Press, Inc.

Published by Silver Burdett Press, Inc., a division of Simon & Schuster, Inc., Englewood Cliffs, N.J. 07632.

Library of Congress Cataloging-in-Publication Data

Klinkner, Philip A.
  The First Amendment/by Philip A. Klinkner: with an introduction
by Warren E. Burger
    p. cm.—(The American Heritage history of the Bill of
Rights)
    Includes bibliographical references and indexes.
    Summary: Studies the historical origins of provisions of the First
Amendment, which guarantees the freedoms of speech, religion,
assembly, and the press.
    1. United States—Constitutional law—Amendments—1st—History
—Juvenile literature. 2. Freedom of religion—United States
—History—Juvenile literature. 3. Freedom of speech—United States
—History—Juvenile literature. 4. Assembly, Right of—United
States—History—Juvenile literature. {1. United States—
Constitutional law—Amendments—1st—History. 2. Freedom of
speech—History. 3. Freedom of religion—History. 4. Assembly,
Right of—History. 5. Freedom of the press—History.} I. Title.
II. Series.
KF4558 1st, K55 1991
342, 73'0853—dc20
{347.302853}
                                                        90-48851
                                                        CIP
                                                        AC

Manufactured in the United States of America.

ISBN 0-382-24179-7 {lib. bdg.}
10 9 8 7 6 5 4 3 2 1

ISBN 0-382-24192-4 {pbk.}
10 9 8 7 6 5 4 3 2 1

CONTENTS

INTRODUCTION

WARREN E. BURGER
Chief Justice of the United States, 1969–1986

The First Amendment is so fundamental to our American way of life that it is sometimes perceived as the Bill of Rights itself. But its concept of individual freedom and liberty—of religion, expression, and collective action—is much broader than that.

Concepts of liberty—the values liberty protects—inspired the Framers of our Constitution and the Bill of Rights to some of their most impassioned eloquence. "Liberty, the greatest of earthly possessions—give us that precious jewel, and you may take everything else," declaimed Patrick Henry. Those toilers in the "vineyard of liberty" sensed the historic nature of their mission, and their foresight accounts for the survival of the Bill of Rights.

Today, courts and citizens alike must consider together many challenging First Amendment issues. Freedom of religion enters into discussions of school prayer, tax credits for church properties, and the right of parents to make choices about their children's education in public or church schools. We continue to refine our definitions of obscenity and censorship. We also struggle with the issue of prior restraint—public officials' power to restrict the use of information—as we try to balance the interests of the valid needs of the military and the role of the media in covering wartime operations.

The long-term success of the system of ordered liberty set up by our Constitution was by no means foreordained. The bicentennial of the Bill of Rights provides an opportunity to reflect on the significance of the freedoms we enjoy and to commit ourselves to exercise the civic responsibilities required to sustain our constitutional system. The Constitution, including its first ten amendments, the Bill of Rights, has survived two centuries because of its unprecedented philosophical premise: that it derives its power from the people. It is not a grant from the government to the people. In 1787 the masters—the people—were saying to their government—their servant—that certain rights are inherent, natural rights and that they belong to the people, who had those rights before any governments existed. The function of government, they said, was to protect these rights.

The Bill of Rights also owes its continued vitality to the fact that it was drafted by experienced, practical politicians. It was a product of the Framers' essential mistrust of the frailties of human nature. This led them to develop the idea of the separation of powers and to make the Bill of Rights part of the permanent Constitution.

Moreover, the document was designed to be flexible, and the role of providing that flexibility through interpretation has fallen to the judiciary. Indeed, the first commander in chief, George Washington, gave the Supreme Court its moral marching orders two centuries ago when he said, "the administration of justice is the firmest pillar of government." The principle of judicial review as a check on government has perhaps nowhere been more significant than in the protection of individual liberties. It has been my privilege, along with my colleagues on the Court, to ensure the continued vitality of our Bill of Rights. As John Marshall asked, long before he became chief justice, "To what quarter will you look for a protection from an infringement on the Constitution, if you will not give the power to the judiciary?"

But the preservation of the Bill of Rights is not the sole responsibility of the judiciary. Rather, judges, legislatures, and presidents are partners with every American; liberty is the responsibility of every public officer and every citizen. In this spirit all Americans should become acquainted with the principles and history of this most remarkable document. Its bicentennial should not be simply a celebration but the beginning of an ongoing process. Americans must—by their conduct—guarantee that it continues to protect the sacred rights of our uniquely multicultural population. We must not fail to exercise our rights to vote, to participate in government and community activities, and to implement the principles of liberty, tolerance, opportunity, and justice for all.

THE AMERICAN HERITAGE
HISTORY OF THE BILL OF RIGHTS

THE FIRST AMENDMENT
by Philip A. Klinkner

THE SECOND AMENDMENT
by Joan C. Hawxhurst

THE THIRD AMENDMENT
by Burnham Holmes

THE FOURTH AMENDMENT
by Paula A. Franklin

THE FIFTH AMENDMENT
by Burnham Holmes

THE SIXTH AMENDMENT
by Eden Force

THE SEVENTH AMENDMENT
by Lila E. Summer

THE EIGHTH AMENDMENT
by Vincent Buranelli

THE NINTH AMENDMENT
by Philip A. Klinkner

THE TENTH AMENDMENT
by Judith Adams

The Bill of Rights

AMENDMENT 1*
Article   Congress shall make no law respecting an establishment of religion, or prohibiting the free exercise thereof; or abridging the freedom of speech, or of the press; or the right of the people peaceably to assemble, and to petition the Government for a redress of grievances.

AMENDMENT 2
Article   A well regulated Militia, being necessary to the security of a free State, the right of the people to keep and bear Arms, shall not be infringed.

AMENDMENT 3
Article   No Soldier shall, in time of peace be quartered in any house, without the consent of the Owner, nor in time of war, but in a manner to be prescribed by law.

AMENDMENT 4
Article   The right of the people to be secure in their persons, houses, papers, and effects, against unreasonable searches and seizures, shall not be violated, and no Warrants shall issue, but upon probable cause, supported by Oath or affirmation, and particularly describing the place to be searched, and the persons or things to be seized.

AMENDMENT 5
Article   No person shall be held to answer for a capital, or otherwise infamous crime, unless on a presentment or indictment of a Grand Jury, except in cases arising in the land or naval forces, or in the Militia, when in actual service in time of War or public danger; nor shall any person be subject for the same offence to be twice put in jeopardy of life or limb; nor shall be compelled in any criminal case to be a witness against himself, nor be deprived of life, liberty, or property, without due process of law; nor shall private property be taken for public use without just compensation.

AMENDMENT 6
Article   In all criminal prosecutions, the accused shall enjoy the right to a speedy and public trial, by an impartial jury of the State and district wherein the crime shall have been committed, which district shall have been previously ascertained by law, and to be informed of the nature and cause of the accusation; to be confronted with the witnesses against him; to have compulsory process for obtaining Witnesses in his favor, and to have the assistance of counsel for his defence.

AMENDMENT 7
Article   In Suits at common law, where the value in controversy shall exceed twenty dollars, the right of trial by jury shall be preserved, and no fact tried by a jury, shall be otherwise reexamined in any Court of the United States, than according to the rules of the common law.

AMENDMENT 8
Article   Excessive bail shall not be required, nor excessive fines imposed, nor cruel and unusual punishments inflicted.

AMENDMENT 9
Article   The enumeration in the Constitution, of certain rights, shall not be construed to deny or disparage others retained by the people.

AMENDMENT 10
Article   The powers not delegated to the United States by the Constitution, nor prohibited by it to the States, are reserved to the States respectively, or to the people.

*Note that each of the first ten amendments to the original Constitution is called an "Article." None of these amendments had actual numbers at the time of their ratification.

1770s–1790s

1774 Quartering Act
1775 Revolutionary War begins
1776 Declaration of Independence is signed.
1783 Revolutionary War ends.
1787 Constitutional Convention writes the U.S. Constitution.
1788 U.S. Constitution is ratified by most states.
1789 Congress proposes the Bill of Rights
1791 The Bill of Rights is ratified by the states.
1792 Militia Act

1800s–1820s

1803 *Marbury* v. *Madison.* Supreme Court declares that it has the power of judicial review and exercises it. This is the first case in which the Court holds a law of Congress unconstitutional.
1807 Trial of Aaron Burr. Ruling that juries may have knowledge of a case so long as they have not yet formed an opinion.
1813 Kentucky becomes the first state to outlaw concealed weapons.
1824 *Gibbons* v. *Ogden.* Supreme Court defines Congress's power to regulate commerce, including trade between states and within states if that commerce affects other states.

1830s–1870s

1833 *Barron* v. *Baltimore*. Supreme Court rules that Bill of Rights applies only to actions of the federal government, not to the states and local governments.

1851 *Cooley* v. *Board of Wardens of the Port of Philadelphia*. Supreme Court rules that states can apply their own rules to some foreign and interstate commerce if their rules are of a local nature—unless or until Congress makes rules for particular situations.

1857 *Dred Scott* v. *Sandford*. Supreme Court denies that African Americans are citizens even if they happen to live in a "free state."

1862 Militia Act

1865 Thirteenth Amendment is ratified. Slavery is not allowed in the United States.

1868 Fourteenth Amendment is ratified. All people born or naturalized in the United States are citizens. Their privileges and immunities are protected, as are their life, liberty, and property according to due process. They have equal protection of the laws.

1873 *Slaughterhouse* cases. Supreme Court rules that the Fourteenth Amendment does not limit state power to make laws dealing with economic matters. Court mentions the unenumerated right to political participation.

1876 *United States* v. *Cruikshank*. Supreme Court rules that the right to bear arms for a lawful purpose is not an absolute right granted by the Constitution. States can limit this right and make their own gun-control laws.

1880s–1920s

1884 *Hurtado* v. *California*. Supreme Court rules that the right to a grand jury indictment doesn't apply to the states.

1896 *Plessy* v. *Ferguson*. Supreme Court upholds a state law based on "separate but equal" facilities for different races.

1903 Militia Act creates National Guard.

1905 *Lochner* v. *New York*. Supreme Court strikes down a state law regulating maximum work hours.

1914 *Weeks* v. *United States*. Supreme Court establishes that illegally obtained evidence, obtained by unreasonable search and seizure, cannot be used in federal trials.

1918 *Hammer* v. *Dagenhart*. Supreme Court declares unconstitutional a federal law prohibiting the shipment between states of goods made by young children.

1923 *Meyer* v. *Nebraska*. Supreme Court rules that a law banning teaching of foreign languages or teaching in languages other than English is unconstitutional. Court says that certain areas of people's private lives are protected from government interference.

1925 *Carroll* v. *United States*. Supreme Court allows searches of automobiles without a search warrant under some circumstances.

1925 *Gitlow* v. *New York*. Supreme Court rules that freedom of speech and freedom of the press are protected from state actions by the Fourteenth Amendment.

1930s

1931 *Near* v. *Minnesota*. Supreme Court rules that liberty of the press and of speech are safeguarded from state action.

1931 *Stromberg* v. *California*. Supreme Court extends concept of freedom of speech to symbolic actions such as displaying a flag.

1932 *Powell* v. *Alabama* (*First Scottsboro* case). Supreme Court rules that poor defendants have a right to an appointed lawyer when tried for crimes that may result in the death penalty.

1934 National Firearms Act becomes the first federal law to restrict the keeping and bearing of arms.

1935 *Norris* v. *Alabama* (*Second Scottsboro* case). Supreme Court reverses the conviction of an African American because of the long continued excluding of African Americans from jury service in the trial area.

1937 *Palko* v. *Connecticut*. Supreme Court refuses to require states to protect people under the double jeopardy clause of the Bill of Rights. But the case leads to future application of individual rights in the Bill of Rights to the states on a case-by-case basis.

1937 *DeJonge* v. *Oregon*. Supreme Court rules that freedom of assembly and petition are protected against state laws.

1939 *United States* v. *Miller*. Supreme Court rules that National Firearms Act of 1934 does not violate Second Amendment.

1940s–1950s

1940 *Cantwell* v. *Connecticut*. Supreme Court rules that free exercise of religion is protected against state laws.

1943 *Barnette* v. *West Virginia State Board of Education*. Supreme Court rules that flag salute laws are unconstitutional.

1946 *Theil* v. *Pacific Railroad*. Juries must be a cross section of the community, excluding no group based on religion, race, sex, or economic status.

1947 *Everson* v. *Board of Education*. Supreme Court rules that government attempts to impose religious practices, the establishment of religion, is forbidden to the states.

1948 *In re Oliver*. Supreme Court rules that defendants have a right to public trial in nonfederal trials.

1949 *Wolf* v. *California*. Supreme Court rules that freedom from unreasonable searches and seizures also applies to states.

1954 *Brown* v. *Board of Education of Topeka*. Supreme Court holds that segregation on the basis of race (in public education) denies equal protection of the laws.

1958 *NAACP* v. *Alabama*. Supreme Court rules that the privacy of membership lists in an organization is part of the right to freedom of assembly and association.

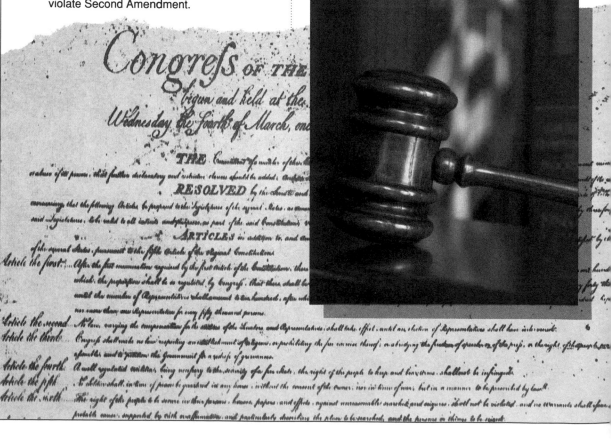

1960s

1961 *Mapp* v. *Ohio*. Supreme Court rules that illegally obtained evidence must not be allowed in state criminal trials.

1962 *Engel* v. *Vitale*. Supreme Court strikes down state-sponsored school prayer, saying it is no business of government to compose official prayers as part of a religious program carried on by the government.

1963 *Gideon* v. *Wainwright*. Supreme Court rules that the right of people accused of serious crimes to be represented by an appointed counsel applies to state criminal trials.

1964 Civil Rights Act is passed.

1964 *Malloy* v. *Hogan*. Supreme Court rules that the right to protection against forced self-incrimination applies to state trials.

1965 *Griswold* v. *Connecticut*. Supreme Court rules that there is a right to privacy in marriage and declares unconstitutional a state law banning the use of or the giving of information about birth control.

1965 *Pointer* v. *Texas*. Supreme Court rules that the right to confront witnesses against an accused person applies to state trials.

1966 *Parker* v. *Gladden*. Supreme Court ruling is interpreted to mean that the right to an impartial jury is applied to the states.

1966 *Miranda* v. *Arizona*. Supreme Court extends the protection against forced self-incrimination. Police have to inform people in custody of their rights before questioning them.

1967 *Katz* v. *United States*. Supreme Court rules that people's right to be free of unreasonable searches includes protection against electronic surveillance.

1967 *Washington* v. *Texas*. Supreme Court rules that accused people have the right to have witnesses in their favor brought into court.

1967 *In re Gault*. Supreme Court rules that juvenile proceedings that might lead to the young person's being sent to a state institution must follow due process and fair treatment. These include the rights against forced self-incrimination, to counsel, to confront witnesses.

1967 *Klopfer* v. *North Carolina*. Supreme Court rules that the right to a speedy trial applies to state trials.

1968 *Duncan* v. *Louisiana*. Supreme Court rules that the right to a jury trial in criminal cases applies to state trials.

1969 *Benton* v. *Maryland*. Supreme Court rules that the protection against double jeopardy applies to the states.

1969 *Brandenburg* v. *Ohio*. Supreme Court rules that speech calling for the use of force or crime can only be prohibited if it is directed to bringing about immediate lawless action and is likely to bring about such action.

1970s–1990s

1970 *Williams* v. *Florida*. Juries in cases that do not lead to the possibility of the death penalty may consist of six jurors rather than twelve.

1971 *Pentagon Papers* case. Freedom of the press is protected by forbidding prior restraint.

1971 *Duke Power Co.* v. *Carolina Environmental Study Group, Inc.* Supreme Court upholds state law limiting liability of federally licensed power companies in the event of a nuclear accident.

1972 *Furman* v. *Georgia*. Supreme Court rules that the death penalty (as it was then decided upon) is cruel and unusual punishment and therefore unconstitutional.

1972 *Argersinger* v. *Hamlin*. Supreme Court rules that right to counsel applies to all criminal cases that might involve a jail term.

1973 *Roe* v. *Wade*. Supreme Court declares that the right to privacy protects a woman's right to end pregnancy by abortion under specified circumstances.

1976 *Gregg* v. *Georgia*. Supreme Court rules that the death penalty is to be allowed if it is decided upon in a consistent and reasonable way, if the sentencing follows strict guidelines, and if the penalty is not required for certain crimes.

1976 *National League of Cities* v. *Usery*. Supreme Court holds that the Tenth Amendment prevents Congress from making federal minimum wage and overtime rules apply to state and city workers.

1981 *Quilici* v. *Village of Morton Grove*. U.S. district court upholds a local ban on sale and possession of handguns.

1985 *Garcia* v. *San Antonio Metropolitan Transit Authority*. Supreme Court rules that Congress can make laws dealing with wages and hour rules applied to city-owned transportation systems.

1989 *Webster* v. *Reproductive Health Services*. Supreme Court holds that a state may prohibit all use of public facilities and publicly employed staff in abortions.

1989 *Johnson* v. *Texas*. Supreme Court rules that flag burning is protected and is a form of "symbolic speech."

1990 *Cruzan* v. *Missouri Department of Health*. Supreme Court recognizes for the first time a very sick person's right to die without being forced to undergo unwanted medical treatment and a person's right to a living will.

1990 *Noriega–CNN* case. Supreme Court upholds lower federal court's decision to allow temporary prior restraint thus limiting the First Amendment right of freedom of the press.

The Birth of the Bill of Rights

"We hold these truths to be self-evident, that all men are created equal, that they are endowed by their Creator with certain unalienable Rights, that among these are Life, Liberty, and the pursuit of Happiness."

THE DECLARATION OF INDEPENDENCE (1776)

A brave Chinese student standing in front of a line of tanks, Eastern Europeans marching against the secret police, happy crowds dancing on top of the Berlin Wall—these were recent scenes of people trying to gain their freedom or celebrating it. The scenes and the events that sparked them will live on in history. They also show the lasting gift that is our Bill of Rights. The freedoms guaranteed by the Bill of Rights have guided and inspired millions of people all over the world in their struggle for freedom.

The Colonies Gain Their Freedom

Like many countries today, the United States fought to gain freedom and democracy for itself. The American colonies had a revolution from 1775 to 1783 to free themselves from British rule.

The colonists fought to free themselves because they believed that the British had violated, or gone against, their rights. The colonists held what some considered the extreme idea that all

James Madison is known as both the "Father of the Constitution" and the "Father of the Bill of Rights." In 1789 he proposed to Congress the amendments that became the Bill of Rights. Madison served two terms as president of the United States from 1809 to 1817.

The Raising of the Liberty Pole by John McRae. In 1776, American colonists hoisted liberty poles as symbols of liberty and freedom from British rule. At the top they usually placed a liberty cap. Such caps resembled the caps given to slaves in ancient Rome when they were freed.

persons are born with certain rights. They believed that these rights could not be taken away, even by the government. The importance our nation gave to individual rights can be seen in the Declaration of Independence. The Declaration, written by Thomas Jefferson in 1776, states:

> We hold these truths to be self-evident, that all men are created equal, that they are endowed by their Creator with certain unalienable Rights, that among these are Life, Liberty, and the pursuit of Happiness.

The United States won its independence from Britain in 1783. But with freedom came the difficult job of forming a government. The Americans wanted a government that was strong enough to keep peace and prosperity, but not so strong that it might take away the rights for which the Revolution had been fought. The Articles of Confederation was the country's first written plan of government.

The Articles of Confederation, becoming law in 1781, created a weak national government. The defects in the Articles soon became clear to many Americans. Because the United States did not have a strong national government, its economy suffered. Under the Articles, Congress did not have the power to tax. It had to ask the states for money or borrow it. There was no separate president or court system. Nine of the states had to agree before Congress's bills became law. In 1786 economic problems caused farmers in Massachusetts to revolt. The national government was almost powerless to stop the revolt. It was also unable to build an army or navy strong enough to protect the United States's borders and its ships on the high seas.

The Constitution Is Drawn Up

The nation's problems had to be solved. So, in February 1787, the Continental Congress asked the states to send delegates to a convention to discuss ways of improving the Articles. That May, fifty-five delegates, from every state except Rhode Island, met in Philadelphia. The group included some of the country's most famous leaders: George Washington, hero of the Revolution; Benjamin Franklin, publisher, inventor, and diplomat; and James Madison, a leading critic of the Articles. Madison would soon become the guiding force behind the Constitutional Convention.

After a long, hot summer of debate the delegates finally drew up the document that became the U.S. Constitution. It set up a strong central government. But it also divided power between three branches of the federal government. These three branches were the executive branch (the presidency), the legislative branch (Congress), and the judicial branch (the courts). Each was given one part of the government's power. This division was to make sure that no single branch became so powerful that it could violate the people's rights.

The legislative branch (made up of the House of Representatives and the Senate) would have the power to pass laws, raise taxes and spend money, regulate the national economy, and declare war. The executive branch was given the power to carry out the laws, run foreign affairs, and command the military.

The Signing of the Constitution painted by Thomas Rossiter. The Constitutional Convention met in Philadelphia from May into September 1787. The proposed Constitution contained protection for some individual rights such as protection against *ex post facto* laws and bills of attainder. When the Constitution was ratified by the required number of states in 1788, however, it did not have a bill of rights.

The role of the judicial branch in this plan was less clear. The Constitution said that the judicial branch would have "judicial power." However, it was unclear exactly what this power was. Over the years "judicial power" has come to mean "judicial review." The power of judicial review allows the federal courts to reject laws passed by Congress or the state legislatures that they believe violate the Constitution.

Judicial review helps protect our rights. It allows federal courts to reject laws that violate the Constitution's guarantees of individual rights. Because of this power, James Madison believed that the courts would be an "impenetrable bulwark," an unbreakable wall, against any attempt by government to take away these rights.

The Constitution did more than divide the power of the federal government among the three branches. It also divided power between the states and the federal government. This division of power is known as *federalism.* Federalism means that the federal

government has control over certain areas. These include regulating the national economy and running foreign and military affairs. The states have control over most other areas. For example, they regulate their economies and make most other laws. Once again, the Framers (writers) of the Constitution hoped that the division of powers would keep both the states and the federal government from becoming too strong and possibly violating individual rights.

The new Constitution did *not,* however, contain a bill of rights. Such a bill would list the people's rights and would forbid the government from interfering with them. The only discussion of the topic came late in the convention. At that time, George Mason of Virginia called for a bill of rights. A Connecticut delegate, Roger Sherman, disagreed. He claimed that a bill of rights was not needed. In his view, the Constitution did not take away any of the rights in the bills of rights in the state constitutions. These had been put in place during the Revolution. The other delegates agreed with Roger Sherman. Mason's proposal was voted down by all.

Yet the Constitution was not without guarantees of individual rights. One of these rights was the protection of *habeas corpus.* This is a legal term that refers to the right of someone who has been arrested to be brought into court and formally charged with a crime. Another right forbade *ex post facto* laws. These are laws that outlaw actions that took place before the passage of the laws. Other parts of the Constitution forbade bills of attainder (laws pronouncing a person guilty of a crime without trial), required jury trials, restricted convictions for treason, and guaranteed a republican form of government. That is a government in which political power rests with citizens who vote for elected officials and representatives responsible to the voters. The Constitution also forbade making public officials pass any "religious test." This meant that religious requirements could not be forced on public officials.

The Debate Over the New Constitution

Once it was written, the Constitution had to be ratified, or approved, by nine of the states before it could go into effect. The new

Constitution created much controversy. Heated battles raged in many states over whether or not to approve the document. One of the main arguments used by those who opposed the Constitution (the Anti-Federalists) was that the Constitution made the federal government too strong. They feared that it might violate the rights of the people just as the British government had. Although he had helped write the Constitution, Anti-Federalist George Mason opposed it for this reason. He claimed that he would sooner chop off his right hand than put it to the Constitution as it then stood.

To correct what they viewed as flaws in the Constitution, the Anti-Federalists insisted that it have a bill of rights. The fiery orator of the Revolution, Patrick Henry, another Anti-Federalist, exclaimed, "Liberty, the greatest of all earthly blessings—give us that precious jewel, and you may take every thing else!"

Although he was not an Anti-Federalist, Thomas Jefferson also believed that a bill of rights was needed. He wrote a letter to James Madison, a wavering Federalist, in which he said: "A bill of rights is what the people are entitled to against every government on earth."

Supporters of the Constitution (the Federalists) argued that it did not need a bill of rights. One reason they stated, similar to that given at the Philadelphia convention, was that most state constitutions had a bill of rights. Nothing in the Constitution would limit or abolish these rights. In 1788 James Madison wrote that he thought a bill of rights would provide only weak "parchment barriers" against attempts by government to take away individual rights. He believed that history had shown that a bill of rights was ineffective on "those occasions when its control [was] needed most."

The views of the Anti-Federalists seem to have had more support than did those of the Federalists. The Federalists came to realize that without a bill of rights, the states might not approve the new Constitution. To ensure ratification, the Federalists therefore agreed to support adding a bill of rights to the Constitution.

With this compromise, eleven of the thirteen states ratified the Constitution by July 1788. The new government of the United States was born. The two remaining states, North Carolina and

Rhode Island, in time accepted the new Constitution. North Carolina approved it in November 1789 and Rhode Island in May 1790.

James Madison Calls for a Bill of Rights

On April 30, 1789, George Washington took the oath of office as president. The new government was launched. One of its first jobs was to amend, or change, the Constitution to include a bill of rights. This is what many of the states had called for during the ratification process. Leading this effort in the new Congress was James Madison. He was a strong supporter of individual rights. As a member of the Virginia legislature, he had helped frame the Virginia Declaration of Rights. He had also fought for religious liberty.

Madison, however, had at first opposed including a bill of rights. But his views had changed. He feared that the Constitution would not be ratified by enough states to become law unless the Federalists offered to include a bill of rights. Madison also knew that many people were afraid of the new government. He feared they might oppose its actions or attempt to undo it. He said a bill of rights "will kill the opposition everywhere, and by putting an end to disaffection to [discontent with] the Government itself, enable the administration to venture on measures not otherwise safe."

On June 8, 1789, the thirty-eight-year-old Madison rose to speak in the House of Representatives. He called for several changes to the Constitution that contained the basis of our present Bill of Rights. Despite his powerful words, Madison's speech did not excite his listeners. Most Federalists in Congress opposed a bill of rights. Others believed that the new Constitution should be given more time to operate before Congress considered making any changes. Many Anti-Federalists wanted a new constitutional convention. There, they hoped to greatly limit the powers of the federal government. These Anti-Federalists thought that adding a bill of rights to the Constitution would prevent their movement for a new convention.

Finally, in August, Madison persuaded the House to consider

his amendments. The House accepted most of them. However, instead of being placed in the relevant sections of the Constitution, as Madison had called for, the House voted to add them as separate amendments. This change—listing the amendments together—made the Bill of Rights the distinct document that it is today.

After approval by the House, the amendments went to the Senate. The Senate dropped what Madison considered the most important part of his plan. This was the protection of freedom of the press, freedom of religious belief, and the right to trial by jury from violation by the states. Protection of these rights from violation by state governments would have to wait until after the Fourteenth Amendment was adopted in 1868.

The House and the Senate at last agreed on ten amendments to protect individual rights. What rights were protected? Here is a partial list:

The First Amendment protects freedom of religion, of speech, of the press, of peaceful assembly, and of petition.

The Second Amendment gives to the states the right to keep a militia (a volunteer, reserve military force) and to the people the right to keep and bear arms.

The Third Amendment prevents the government from keeping troops in private homes during wartime.

The Fourth Amendment protects individuals from unreasonable searches and seizures by the government.

The Fifth Amendment states that the government must get an indictment (an official ruling that a crime has been committed) before someone can be tried for a serious crime. This amendment bans "double jeopardy." This means trying a person twice for the same criminal offense. It also protects people from having to testify against themselves in court.

The Fifth Amendment also says that the government cannot take away a person's "life, liberty, or property, without due process of law." This means that the government must follow fair and just procedures if it takes away a person's "life, liberty, or property." Finally, the Fifth Amendment says that if the government takes property from an individual for public use, it must pay that person an adequate sum of money for the property.

The Sixth Amendment requires that all criminal trials be speedy and public, and decided by a fair jury. The amendment also allows people on trial to know what offense they have been charged with. It also allows them to be present when others testify against them, to call witnesses to their defense, and to have the help of a lawyer.

The Seventh Amendment provides for a jury trial in all cases involving amounts over $20.

The Eighth Amendment forbids unreasonably high bail (money paid to free someone from jail before his or her trial), unreasonably large fines, and cruel and unusual punishments.

The Ninth Amendment says that the rights of the people are not limited only to those listed in the Bill of Rights.

Finally, the Tenth Amendment helps to establish federalism by giving to the states and the people any powers not given to the federal government by the Constitution.

After being approved by the House and the Senate, the amendments were sent to the states for adoption in October 1789. By December 1791, three-fourths of the states had approved the ten amendments we now know as the Bill of Rights. The Bill of Rights had become part of the U.S. Constitution.

How Our Court System Works

Many of the events in this book concern court cases involving the Bill of Rights. To help understand how the U.S. court system works, here is a brief description.

The U.S. federal court system has three levels. At the lowest level are the federal district courts. There are ninety-four district courts, each covering a different area of the United States and its territories. Most cases having to do with the Constitution begin in the district courts.

People who lose their cases in the district courts may then appeal to the next level in the court system, the federal courts of appeals. To appeal means to take your case to a higher court in an attempt to change the lower court's decision. Here, those who are making the appeal try to obtain a different judgment. There are thirteen federal courts of appeals in the United States.

People who lose in the federal courts of appeals may then take their case to the U.S. Supreme Court. It is the highest court in the land. The Supreme Court has the final say in a case. You cannot appeal a Supreme Court decision.

The size of the Supreme Court is set by Congress and has changed over the years. Since 1869 the Supreme Court has been made up of nine justices. One is the chief justice of the United States, and eight are associate justices. The justices are named by the president and confirmed by the Senate.

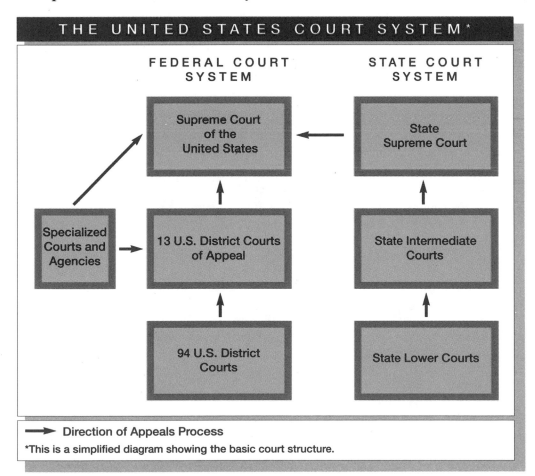

THE UNITED STATES COURT SYSTEM*

FEDERAL COURT SYSTEM

STATE COURT SYSTEM

Supreme Court of the United States

State Supreme Court

Specialized Courts and Agencies

13 U.S. District Courts of Appeal

State Intermediate Courts

94 U.S. District Courts

State Lower Courts

➡ Direction of Appeals Process

*This is a simplified diagram showing the basic court structure.

In the Supreme Court, a simple majority of votes is needed to decide a case. If there is a tie, the lower court's decision remains in effect. When the chief justice votes on the majority side, he or she can assign the writing of the opinion to any of the majority justices, including himself or herself. The opinion states the Court's decision and the reasons for it. Who writes the opinion when the chief justice hasn't voted on the majority side? In that case, the longest-serving associate justice who voted for the majority decision can assign the writing to any of the majority justices, including himself or herself.

What if a justice has voted for the majority decision but doesn't agree with the reasons given in the majority opinion? He or she may write what is called a concurring opinion. That is one which agrees with the Court's decision but for different reasons.

Those justices who disagree with the Court's decision may write what is called a dissenting opinion. They have the opportunity to explain why they think the majority Supreme Court decision is wrong.

In addition to the federal court system, each state has its own system of courts. These systems vary from state to state. However, they are usually made up of two or three levels of lower courts and then the state's highest court, usually called the state supreme court. Those who lose their cases in the state supreme court may appeal those decisions to the federal court system, usually to the Supreme Court.

Not all cases that are appealed to the Supreme Court are heard by it. In fact, very few of them are. For the Supreme Court to decide to hear a case, four of the nine justices must vote to hear it. If fewer than four justices vote to hear the case, then the judgment of the lower court remains in effect.

The First Amendment

The First Amendment protects many of the rights Americans think of first when the Bill of Rights is mentioned—freedom of religion, freedom of the press, freedom of speech, and freedom to assemble peacefully and to petition. Yet over the past two hundred years many controversies have swirled around this amendment. What does the wording actually mean? How far can citizens go in practicing these rights? What happens when an individual's rights conflict with the rights of others? The answers to these questions have changed as the United States has changed.

CHAPTER 1

The Meaning of the First Amendment

"If there is any fixed star in our constitutional constellation, it is that no official, high or petty, can prescribe what shall be orthodox in politics, nationalism, religion, or other matters of opinion or force citizens to confess by word or act their faith therein."

JUSTICE ROBERT JACKSON, in *West Virginia State Board of Education v. Barnette* (1943)

One day in 1935 a third-grade class in Lynn, Massachusetts, stood up to say the Pledge of Allegiance to the U.S. flag. But Carleton Nicholls, Jr., kept his seat. He refused to join his classmates in the pledge. His simple act began one of the most important events in the history of the First Amendment.

Carleton Nicholls, Jr., and his family were Jehovah's Witnesses. The Witnesses are a religious group who think saluting or pledging allegiance to the flag is a sin. They believe that such actions go against the biblical commandment forbidding people to worship anyone or anything but God.

In 1935 Judge Joseph F. Rutherford, the leader of the Jehovah's Witnesses, began a campaign against compulsory, or forced, flag salutes and pledges in school classrooms. Many Witnesses had already been sent to concentration camps in Hitler's Germany for refusing to salute the Nazi flag. Judge Rutherford said Witnesses "do not 'Heil Hitler' nor any other creature."

The statue of Justice on the Supreme Court Building. In her left hand, she holds the scales of justice to weigh both sides before reaching a decision. In her right hand, she holds the sword of punishment. Justice is blind, meaning that decisions are made without being influenced by unrelated issues.

Carleton had heard Judge Rutherford criticize the pledge in a speech. He then decided to refuse to pledge or salute the flag. For this he was sent home from school. Massachusetts had a law that required students to salute the flag. When Carleton's father took him to school the next day, the father also refused to salute the flag. Mr. Nicholls was then arrested for disturbing the peace.

In 1935 many Americans looked upon the reciting of the Pledge of Allegiance as necessary for teaching patriotism to schoolchildren. But the idea of a pledge was very new. The early leaders of our nation opposed the idea of forcing people to take oaths or recite pledges of allegiance. In 1778 George Washington wrote about oaths, "I would not wish in any instance, that there should be the least degree of compulsion [force] exercised." He believed people should give allegiance according to their beliefs, not according to the law.

Attitudes about pledging allegiance began to change by the end of the 1800s. In 1892 the editors of *Youth's Companion* (a magazine) decided that children across the United States should celebrate the 400th anniversary of Columbus's discovery of America by pledging allegiance to the flag. They then published a pledge that went, "I pledge allegiance to my flag and the Republic for which it stands: one nation indivisible, with liberty and justice for all."

The Pledge of Allegiance soon became very popular. Many schools began to use it every day. In 1907 Kansas became the first state to require saying the pledge in its public schools. By 1935 forty states had similar laws. Many other school districts used the pledge even if not required to by state laws.

The incident with the Nicholls family enraged the Jehovah's Witnesses. Judge Rutherford gave a radio speech in which he praised Carleton and his family and criticized compulsory flag salute laws. He stated that "Jehovah's Witnesses conscientiously object [follow their consciences] and refuse to salute the flag and pledge allegiance to it."

Two of the people listening to Judge Rutherford on the radio were William and Lillian Gobitis, fifth- and seventh-grade students in Minersville, Pennsylvania. Like their parents, William and

William and Lillian Gobitis with their father, Walter Gobitis. In *Minersville School District* v. *Gobitis,* the Supreme Court upheld a lower court decision that the local school district could require all children to salute the American flag as part of a daily school exercise.

Lillian were Jehovah's Witnesses. After hearing the story of Carleton Nicholls, William and Lillian wondered if they, too, should refuse to salute the flag. Like any other students, they worried about what their friends and teachers would think. According to Lillian, "I was class president in the seventh grade, and I had good grades. And I felt that, Oh, if I stop saluting the flag, I will blow all this!"

After much thought Lillian and William decided to stand up for what they believed was right. For them this was more important than what their teachers and friends thought. Lillian said later:

So I knew this was the moment! This wasn't something my parents forced on us. They were very firm about that, that what you do is your decision, and you should understand what you're doing. I did a lot of reading and checking in the Bible and I really took my own stand.

Lillian went to school the next day and told her teacher about her decision. Her teacher hugged her and praised her for her courage. Lillian's classmates did not act as kindly. They threw pebbles at her and teased her.

The Minersville school board had a meeting to decide what to do about William and Lillian, and Edmund Wasliewski, who had also refused to salute the flag. William and Lillian's father, Walter Gobitis, went to the meeting and explained why saluting the flag violated their religion. Dr. Charles Roudabush, the school superintendent, did not accept Walter Gobitis's argument, and the board voted to expel the children from school. Walter Gobitis promised, "I'm going to take you to court for this!"

Mr. Gobitis kept his promise. He took the Minersville school board to federal court in February 1938. He argued that by forcing his children to salute the flag, the school board had denied them their right to the free exercise of religion as guaranteed in the First Amendment. Both Lillian and William stated that they loved and respected their country, but their religion told them they could not salute the flag.

The school board understood the First Amendment differently. The board respected William and Lillian's right to practice their religion outside school. But inside school it was another matter. The children would have to follow school rules. The board believed that requiring students to recite the Pledge of Allegiance was necessary to teach respect for the flag. Dr. Roudabush said, "We feel that every citizen and every child in the public schools should have the proper regard for the emblem of the country, the flag." He also claimed that if children could refuse to salute the flag then disrespectful and unpatriotic attitudes might soon take over.

For months the Gobitises waited for the court's decision. Finally, in June 1938 Federal District Judge Albert B. Maris ruled that the school board had denied William and Lillian Gobitis their First Amendment right to free exercise of religion. The case then went to the U.S. Court of Appeals in Philadelphia. The appeals court also ruled that William and Lillian could return to school and that they did not have to salute the flag.

The Minersville school board appealed the case to the U.S. Supreme Court. Since the other courts had agreed with the Gobitis family, the family felt sure that the Supreme Court would rule in their favor. Then one day in June 1940, the Gobitises heard that the Supreme Court had decided against them.

The Supreme Court's Decision

By a vote of 8 to 1, the Supreme Court ruled that schools could require children to take part in flag salutes. Justice Felix Frankfurter said that the *Gobitis* case involved balancing freedom of religion with the need to create patriotism and unity. Frankfurter took a conservative stand on most issues. He believed that unelected judges should usually follow the decisions of elected officials such as lawmakers.

According to Justice Frankfurter, the Minersville school board had decided that the need for national unity was more important than the rights of William and Lillian Gobitis. He worried that if Lillian and William did not have to salute the flag then it "might cast doubts in the minds of the other children" and could lead to disloyalty and, ultimately, disunity. Such a result was dangerous since, in Frankfurter's words, "National unity is the basis of national security."

Justice Harlan Fiske Stone cast the only vote for William and Lillian. He disagreed with Justice Frankfurter's idea that the Supreme Court should leave questions about First Amendment rights to Congress and state and local legislatures. Justice Stone believed that the courts were the only protection minorities had from persecution by the majority.

To make his point even stronger, Justice Stone read his dissenting opinion out loud instead of just handing out written copies. Speaking to the audience, he said that the role of the Constitution

Associate Justice Felix Frankfurter served on the Supreme Court from 1939 to 1962. He was a leader of those who believed in judicial restraint—that judges should not permit their own personal views to influence their decisions when their views do not agree with existing laws and Court decisions.

was to protect the rights of individuals, not government. He went on to say:

> The very essence [basis] of the liberty which they [the Bill of Rights] guarantee is the freedom of the individual from compulsion as to what he shall think and what he shall say, at least where the compulsion is to bear false witness to his religion.

At the time the Supreme Court gave its decision in the *Gobitis* case many people feared for the safety of the country. World War II was being fought. Hitler's armies seemed unstoppable as they marched across Europe. It seemed only a matter of time before the

United States would be at war. For a nation at war, the flag would provide a symbol of patriotism and unity in a difficult time.

Fear of war made some people confuse disagreement with disloyalty. They became suspicious of anyone they thought was unpatriotic. Such a person might be branded as a spy or a traitor. For some Americans, the Supreme Court's ruling was proof that the Witnesses were "un-American" and should be punished.

In the months following the decision in the *Gobitis* case, Jehovah's Witnesses became victims of violence across the country. Investigators for the U.S. Department of Justice kept track of the attacks on Witnesses. They counted more than 300 attacks on Witnesses following the Supreme Court's decision. Their reports included the following:

- In Kennebunk, Maine, angry residents burned a Witness meeting hall to the ground.
- The police in Rockville, Maryland, helped a mob to break up a meeting of Witnesses.
- State troopers had to be called in to Litchfield, Illinois, to protect sixty Witnesses from violence. One Witness was beaten until he agreed to kiss the flag.
- A group of Witnesses was arrested in Connersville, Indiana. A crowd beat them and their lawyers and drove them from town.
- A mob in Jackson, Mississippi, ran a group of Witnesses out of town.

The worst attack came in Richwood, West Virginia. Richwood's sheriff, Martin Louis Catlette, forced nine Witnesses to swallow large doses of castor oil, which causes severe stomach pain and internal bleeding. He then had the Witnesses tied together with a rope and taken out into an angry crowd of hundreds of people. The Witnesses were placed before a flagpole flying the flag. Sheriff Catlette spoke to the crowd:

For God and country we associate ourselves together for the following purposes: To uphold and defend the Constitution of the United States of America, to maintain law and order; . . . to promote the peace and good will on earth; to safeguard and transmit to posterity the principles of justice, freedom and democracy.

Sheriff Catlette and the crowd then began to recite the Pledge of Allegiance. The Witnesses feared for their lives, but they refused to go against their beliefs. The crowd spat on them and called them Nazis. No one in the crowd realized that Witnesses in Germany had suffered similar attacks for refusing to obey the Nazis. None in the crowd seemed to realize that they were the ones who acted like Nazis, not the Witnesses.

Sheriff Catlette then led the crowd as they drove the Witnesses out to the city limits. The Witnesses' cars, which had been damaged and painted over with Nazi swastikas, followed behind. The mob booed as the Witnesses drove out of town in their battered autos.

Despite public resentment against the Witnesses, many people opposed the Supreme Court's ruling. More than one hundred newspaper editorials criticized the Supreme Court for not protecting religious liberty. First Lady Eleanor Roosevelt spoke out against the attacks on the Witnesses.

Many legal and political science journals attacked Justice Felix Frankfurter's opinion. They said that it turned away from the historic role of the courts as the protector of minority rights and gave the go-ahead to the anti-Witness violence. Two Justice Department officials who looked into the attacks on Witnesses wrote, "In short, public health, safety, and morals have not been fortified [strengthened] by the compulsory flag salute laws. Indeed, the result has been quite the contrary."

The attacks on Witnesses and the criticism of the Court's decision led some Supreme Court justices to rethink their opinion. In 1942 three justices who had at first agreed with the flag salute laws stated that they had changed their minds. Justices William O.

Douglas, Hugo Black, and Frank Murphy wrote that the *Gobitis* case had been "wrongly decided."

The decision of these three justices to switch their votes—if they had to decide a new but similar case—along with the vote of Justice Stone meant that now at least four of the nine members of the Supreme Court were willing to outlaw compulsory flag salute laws. Also, two justices who had voted against the Gobitis children had retired. They were replaced by Justices Robert Jackson and Wiley Rutledge. These two justices were more liberal than their predecessors. These changes made it likely that the Court would overturn the decision in the *Gobitis* case.

Another Flag Salute Case

Sensing the chance to score a victory, the Witnesses decided to bring another flag salute case to court. In 1942 West Virginia passed a law requiring flag salutes in its public schools. In Charleston, West Virginia, a young Witness named Marie Barnette was expelled from school for refusing to salute the flag after the law went into effect. According to Marie:

> My older sister, my cousins, and I were going to school right on the edge of Charleston and when the flag exercise was begun, the school didn't even have a flag. So they put up a picture of a flag. When we refused to salute it, they brought in a real flag to see if that would make any difference. We still refused.
>
> Our saluting didn't make any difference to our teacher. She understood. But the principal of the school was the one who kept pressing the matter. He forced the teacher to send us home. The day after that happened, we went back to school, but when we still refused to salute the flag, they sent us home again. This kept happening. We'd go to school; they'd send us home, and we'd go back the next morning. We really tried to go to school.

Eventually the school board suspended and fined Marie and the others for skipping school. Their parents decided to take the case to

The First Amendment
court. Helping them were Judge Rutherford, the leader of the Witnesses, and the American Civil Liberties Union (ACLU), an organization devoted to fighting for First Amendment rights.
The case first went to a federal appeals court in September 1942. The Barnettes' arguments were similar to those made by the Gobitises. They claimed the West Virginia law was unconstitutional because it forced them to go against their religious beliefs. The West Virginia State Board of Education claimed that flag salutes were needed to teach patriotism.
The federal appeals court's three judges all agreed that the West Virginia Law was unconstitutional. They claimed that forcing Witnesses to go against their religious beliefs by saluting the flag was "tyranny." In their words, "This court will not countenance [allow] such tyranny, but will use the power at its command to see that rights guaranteed by the fundamental law [the Constitution] are respected."
The Barnette case then went to the U.S. Supreme Court. The Court handed down its decision on June 14, 1943. It was an important day for this decision—Flag Day.
Three justices still believed that flag salute laws were constitutional. In their dissent in West Virginia State Board of Education v. Barnette, they said that the Supreme Court should let elected officials decide these issues. Once again Justice Felix Frankfurter wrote the opinion for this side.
Before becoming a Supreme Court justice, Felix Frankfurter had been a famous professor at Harvard Law School. As a founder of the American Civil Liberties Union (ACLU) he had fought for free speech. Justice Frankfurter was also a Jew who had been born in Vienna, Austria. He was painfully aware of the persecution suffered by Jews because of their religion. His uncle had only recently escaped from Nazi rule in Austria.
Justice Frankfurter's opinion reveals the dilemma he faced. He wrote that as a member of "the most vilified [slandered] and persecuted minority in history" he would like to have agreed with William and Lillian Gobitis and Marie Barnette. But he believed

that as a Supreme Court justice he could not let his personal views get in the way of the law. The law of the Constitution, Frankfurter believed, required that unelected courts should not tell local school boards and state legislatures how to run their classrooms.

The six other justices voted to ban, or forbid, compulsory flag salute laws. One of these justices was Harlan Fiske Stone, the lone dissenter in the *Gobitis* case and now the chief justice of the United States. With him were the three justices who had changed their mind since the decision in the *Gobitis* case: Black, Douglas, and Murphy. Finally, there were the two new justices, Wiley B. Rutledge and Robert H. Jackson.

Though the Court had finally agreed with his lonely stand, Chief Justice Stone did not write the majority opinion of the Court. He gave that task to Justice Robert Jackson. Justice Jackson's opinion stands out as one of the most powerful defenses of personal liberty in American history.

Justice Robert Jackson wrote that forcing the Jehovah's Witnesses to speak an oath to the flag violated their rights to free speech and religion as much as if they had been forced into silence:

> To sustain [support] the compulsory flag salute we are required to say that a Bill of Rights which guards the individual's right to speak his own mind, left it open to public authorities to compel him to utter what is not in his mind.

Jackson did not agree with Frankfurter's belief that questions about flag salutes should be left to elected officials:

> The very purpose of the Bill of Rights was to withdraw certain subjects from the vicissitudes of political controversy, to place them beyond the reach of majorities and officials and to establish them as legal principles to be applied by the courts. One's rights to life, liberty, and property, to free speech, a free press, freedom of worship and assembly, and other fundamental rights may not be submitted to vote; they depend on the outcome of no elections.

Harlan Fiske Stone served on the Supreme Court from 1925 to 1946.

Jackson then said that it was both necessary and proper for public schools to teach patriotism and unity, especially since the nation was then fighting World War II. However, he argued, *forcing* unity would make the United States no different from its enemies, such as Nazi Germany, that had achieved unity by violence and fear. He wrote, "Those who begin coercive [forced] elimination of dissent soon find themselves exterminating [wiping out] dissenters. Compulsory unification of opinion achieves only the unanimity [total agreement] of the graveyard." Jackson concluded by saying that forcing unity was contrary to the meaning of the Constitution:

> If there is any fixed star in our constitutional constellation, it is that no official, high or petty [low], can prescribe what shall be orthodox [accepted] in politics, nationalism, religion, or other matters of opinion or force citizens to confess by word or act their faith therein.

The "fixed star" that Justice Jackson spoke of is found in the First Amendment. The First Amendment states:

> Congress shall make no law respecting an establishment of religion, or prohibiting the free exercise thereof; or abridging the freedom of speech, or of the press; or the right of the people peaceably to assemble, and to petition the Government for a redress of grievances.

In short, this amendment guarantees freedom of expression—the freedom to think what we wish and to express those thoughts publicly. Because of the First Amendment, we, the people, are free to decide what to say and believe.

Of all the rights we have as Americans and as humans, freedom of expression is perhaps the most important. As Supreme Court Justice Hugo Black said:

> Freedom to speak and write about public questions is as important to the life of government as is the heart of the human body. In fact, this privilege is the heart of our government! If that heart be weakened, the result is debilitation [crippling]; if it be stilled, the result is death.

Freedom of expression is the cornerstone of a democracy. If democracy means that the people rule, then the people must have the right to hear all sides of an argument and to state their opinions on important matters. Only in this way can the people control the government.

The freedoms guaranteed in the First Amendment, enforced by our courts, also help to protect members of unpopular minorities, like William and Lillian Gobitis, from persecution. Again, Justice Black stated this well when he said:

> Under our constitutional system, courts stand against any winds that blow as havens of refuge for those who might otherwise suffer because they are helpless, weak, outnumbered, or because they are non-conforming victims of prejudice and public excitement.

No right is absolute. People disagree over how much freedom the rights in the First Amendment give us. But most people agree that the First Amendment has helped to protect some of our most valued liberties. Justice Jackson compared the First Amendment to a star. Just as sailors are guided by the stars in the sky, the First Amendment has helped show the way to the many freedoms we Americans enjoy.

The Birth of the First Amendment

"We shall find that the censorial power is in the people over the Government, and not in the Government over the people."

JAMES MADISON, 1794

The Founders of our nation understood the importance of free expression. They showed this by placing a guarantee of free expression at the beginning of our Bill of Rights. They believed that only if the people knew of the activities of the government, especially its mistakes, could they control it. The author of the Bill of Rights, James Madison, said that in the new government, "we shall find that the censorial power [the power to stop something] is in the people over the Government, and not in the Government over the people."

The Founders were very aware of the past. They knew how the English government years before had placed limits on the right of the people to freely express their views. At one time in England, criticizing the monarch was considered seditious. This means that it might cause rebellion. The punishment for sedition was jail and the loss of all property for the first offense, life imprisonment for the second offense, and death for the third offense.

A Quaker trial. The Quakers were one of the religious groups persecuted in the 1600s in England. In 1682, William Penn founded the colony of Pennsylvania as a safe place for Quakers to live and worship. When Pennsylvania became a state, citizens made sure that their state's declaration of rights protected the free exercise of religion.

The English government was even more harsh to those who printed seditious materials. A book or a pamphlet has the potential to stir up trouble far longer than spoken words. That is because it can be printed in large numbers and given out freely. To make sure that no one printed anything critical of the government, the English Parliament in 1558 made it illegal to publish any document without the approval of the government. Anyone caught with forbidden books could be put to death.

In 1663, John Twyn, a printer, published a banned book that claimed King Charles II should be held responsible to the people. The English government considered ideas like this to be treason. The authorities promised not to execute Twyn if he gave the name of the book's author. He refused to do so, saying, "Better one suffer, than many." Twyn was beheaded for his stand.

The English government also punished religious dissenters who questioned the rule of the Church of England, the official religion. Many members of various religious groups fled England to the American colonies to escape persecution. The Puritans of New England, Quakers of Pennsylvania, and Roman Catholics of Maryland were all refugees from religious oppression in England.

Attacks on the people's right of free expression also took place in the British-ruled American colonies. In many colonies printers needed permission from the government to publish documents. Often publishers went to jail for printing items critical of the government. Even Benjamin Franklin's brother James was among those jailed.

Most colonies also lacked freedom of religion. The worst examples of religious intolerance were in Puritan New England. In Massachusetts and Connecticut, only members of the Puritan church could vote or hold public office. Laws in these colonies required all persons, whether Puritans or not, to pay taxes to support the Puritan church. The Puritans gathered up "blasphemous" books (those they considered critical of God) and burned them in public. Members of religious minorities were often the victims of violence in the Puritan-controlled colonies. Quakers in New England were branded with irons and had their ears cut off.

Other colonies were more tolerant of different religious views. Rhode Island, Pennsylvania, and Maryland were all established as safe places for religious minorities. Rhode Island even guaranteed freedom of religion for non-Christians.

There were also examples of freedom of the press in the American colonies. One example is the trial of John Peter Zenger held during 1734 and 1735. Zenger published a newspaper in New York City that criticized the royal governor, William Cosby. Zenger accused Cosby of violating the rights of the people. Cosby had Zenger arrested for "raising sedition" among the public and "inflaming their Minds with contempt" of His Majesty's Government, and greatly disturbing the peace.

Zenger's attorney, Andrew Hamilton, thought the case was crucial to the idea of liberty in the colonies. He asked the jury not to convict Zenger since what his client had printed was true. In a stirring appeal, Hamilton said:

> The question before the court and you gentlemen of the jury is not of small nor private concern. It is not the cause of the poor printer, nor of New York alone, which you are now trying. No! It may in its consequence affect every freeman that lives under a British government on the main of America. It is the best cause. It is the cause of Liberty.

The jury found John Peter Zenger innocent. His case helped to establish freedom of the press in the colonies.

Bills of Rights

The abuse of rights by the British before the Revolution made Americans even more sensitive to the need to protect them. Freedoms of speech, press, and religion found their way into many state constitutions. These were written during the American Revolution. Virginia adopted the most famous of these constitutions in 1776. The Virginia Declaration of Rights, drafted mainly by George Mason and James Madison, guaranteed freedom of the

The burning of John Peter Zenger's newspaper in Wall Street, New York City, in 1734. The colonial government lost its case against him. Zenger's victory was an important victory for freedom of the press.

press and of religion. Pennsylvania's constitution also included protection of free speech. In time eight states adopted bills of rights.

Although some states had bills of rights, the Framers did not see the need to include a bill of rights in the U.S. Constitution. Later the Federalists agreed to include a bill of rights. They did this mainly to make sure that the states would approve the Constitution. The task of drawing up a bill of rights fell to James Madison. A staunch Federalist, Madison at first opposed placing a bill of rights in the Constitution. He was, however, a strong supporter of the right to free expression. And as a Virginia state legislator, he helped frame the Virginia Declaration of Rights. Madison had also successfully fought against an attempt to pass a tax to support a state religion.

Madison overcame his earlier doubts and supported a bill of rights. He believed a bill of rights would protect people's freedoms from the government. Madison thought a bill of rights would safeguard unpopular minorities, since the greatest danger to liberty came from "the body of the people, operating by the majority against the minority."

One of Madison's proposed amendments stated, "The civil rights of none shall be abridged [lessened] on account of religious belief or worship, nor shall any national religion be established, nor shall the full and equal rights of conscience be in any manner, or on any pretext, abridged." The House and the Senate changed Madison's wording. They also added guarantees of the freedom of speech, the freedom of the press, and the right of people to peacefully assemble and to petition. The final product became the First Amendment as we know it today.

Madison also included an amendment that said, "No state shall infringe the equal rights of conscience, nor the freedom of speech, or of the press, nor of the right to trial by jury in criminal cases." Since the other amendments seemed to apply only to the federal government, such an amendment would have kept the states from denying many of the liberties protected by the First Amendment. Though Madison believed that this was "the most valuable amendment in the whole list," the Senate rejected it. Protection from state governments' infringement of individual rights would have to wait until after the ratification of the Fourteenth Amendment in 1866.

Madison persuaded a reluctant Congress to approve the amendments. Congress then sent the amendments to the states for ratification, or approval. After approval by three-fourths of the states, the Bill of Rights became law in December 1791.

Ratification did not end discussion of the Bill of Rights and the First Amendment. Many questions remained. Would the Bill of Rights really work, or would it only provide a useless "parchment barrier" against government repression? What was meant by the beginning phrase in the First Amendment: "Congress shall make no law . . ."? Were the rights protected by this amendment untouchable? Or could they be limited in the interest of the national welfare? Did these protections apply only to the federal government? Or would they also prohibit the states from violating freedom of expression? Only time would provide an answer to these questions.

CHAPTER 3

Freedom of Expression:
From 1798 to 1900

"I do not admit that it is the business of this assembly to decide whether
I shall or shall not publish a newspaper in this city. . . . Before God and
you all, I here pledge myself to continue it, if need be till death."

ELIJAH LOVEJOY, 1837

Soon after the adoption of the First Amendment in 1791, Americans were forced to struggle with its meaning. The first test of the First Amendment came in 1798. The new nation was still very young, and there were many debates over how it should be run.

One of the most important debates was over foreign policy. The nation was divided over which side to support in a war between France and Great Britain. They were the two most powerful nations in the world at that time. The Federalist party, led by President John Adams and Alexander Hamilton, favored Britain. They knew that the United States relied heavily on trade with Britain.

On the other side was the Democratic-Republican party. It was led by Thomas Jefferson and James Madison. They opposed supporting Great Britain in the war. After all, they argued, France had helped the United States in its revolution against Britain. The Democratic-Republicans used this issue to stir up opposition to Federalist policies.

To stamp out criticism of its policies, the Federalist majority in Congress passed the Sedition Act in 1798. This law made it a crime

---

John Adams, the second president of the United States, was a leading Federalist. During his administration, Congress passed the Sedition Act.

to "write, print, utter [speak], or publish . . . any false, scandalous and malicious [mean and spiteful] writings against the government of the United States." Even the mildest criticism of the government could result in a heavy fine or jail term. More than twenty-five people went to jail for breaking the law. The law kept many others from stating their opinions for fear of punishment.

The Sedition Act angered many Americans. Thomas Jefferson said the law created a "reign of terror." The dislike of the law helped Jefferson defeat Adams in the presidential election of 1800. Once elected, Jefferson pardoned those sent to jail under the act, and Congress gave back the fines that were paid.

Many people, including James Madison, believed that the Sedition Act violated the First Amendment. Madison had hoped that the Supreme Court would act as an "impenetrable bulwark" against laws like the Sedition Act. His hope was not realized. The Supreme Court never ruled on the Sedition Act. However, several of the Court's members, acting in their roles as lower court judges, upheld it.

Violations of the Freedom of Expression

During the nation's early history the First Amendment was rarely discussed. The Bill of Rights protects people only against the federal government's violation of their rights. And until the 1900s the federal government was small in size and did little that might have violated individual rights.

Before the 1900s, most power was in the hands of the state governments. The states often used their power in ways that violated or restricted individual rights. But the First Amendment did not protect against this. When he drew up the Bill of Rights, Madison had put forth an amendment that would have protected some rights in the First Amendment from interference by states. But this plan had been turned down by the Senate.

In 1833 the Supreme Court strengthened this limit on the Bill of Rights in the case of *Barron* v. *Baltimore*. All the justices of the

Supreme Court voted that the states did not have to follow the Bill of Rights. Chief Justice John Marshall wrote that the Bill of Rights "contain[s] no expression indicating an intention to apply them [the amendments] to the state governments. This court cannot so apply them."

Without the protection of the First Amendment, many saw the state governments violate their religious liberties. Roman Catholic immigrants found that many states kept them from voting or holding office. Some states forced them to pay taxes to support Protestant churches. Catholics and members of other religious minorities also faced discrimination in jobs and schools because of their religion.

The worst example of how state laws restricted individual liberties was in the case of slavery. The Constitution and the Bill of Rights did nothing to protect African-American slaves. The Constitution even considered a slave to be only three-fifths of a person. In its decision in the *Dred Scott* case in 1857, the Supreme Court ruled that slaves were not citizens and therefore had none of the rights essential to human dignity. Slaves were often bought and sold, cruelly overworked, and torn from their families. Attempts by slaves to protest their condition usually brought brutal beatings, torture, and even death.

Beginning in the 1830s many Americans, in both the North and the South, began to call for the abolition, or end, of slavery. The abolitionists, as opponents of slavery were called, met fierce resistance. They saw their rights attacked. Every Southern state had laws against speaking out against slavery. Southern postmasters often stopped antislavery pamphlets from being sent in the mail.

Even in the North, many suffered for their opposition to slavery. The Reverend Elijah Lovejoy published an antislavery journal in Alton, Illinois. Lovejoy's opponents destroyed his press three times. In 1837 the city of Alton stated that the First Amendment did not protect him.

Still Lovejoy continued. He wrote, "I do not admit that it is the business of this assembly to decide whether I shall or shall not

Elijah P. Lovejoy was shot and killed by a mob while trying to protect his printing press. The mob destroyed his printing plant in Alton, Illinois, in 1837. They were angered by the antislavery editorials in his newspaper. He was known as the "Martyr Abolitionist."

publish a newspaper in this city. . . . Before God and you all, I here pledge myself to continue it, if need be till death." Lovejoy's pledge came true. In November 1837, a mob shot and killed Lovejoy as he tried to bring his fourth press into town.

The Civil War Debate Over the First Amendment

The debate over slavery helped ignite the Civil War in 1861. The war brought an end to slavery and established the power of the federal government over the states. The war also led to many Americans being denied their civil liberties. Thousands of people who spoke out against the war were arrested. President Abraham Lincoln and others argued that these restrictions were needed in time of war and rebellion. They claimed that the First Amendment did not permit disloyal speech, since it might destroy the government. They saw it as necessary to violate one part of the Constitution to save the rest.

Others argued that the First Amendment says "Congress shall make no law," *not* "Congress shall make no law in times of peace." They believed that the First Amendment applied at all times—in peacetime and wartime. Otherwise, they argued, the government could always imagine some threat to justify the denial of rights.

President Lincoln and his supporters won the debate. The courts upheld most of the government's actions during the Civil War. Yet, the debate over the balance between the needs for national security and the First Amendment would continue. World War I, World War II, the Korean War, and the war in Vietnam all brought new questions about the limits of our First Amendment rights.

The Civil War finally ended in 1865. After the war the government did away with slavery and gave African Americans citizenship. Congress passed and the states approved three amendments to the Constitution to accomplish this task. The Thirteenth Amendment (1865) abolished slavery in the United States. The Fourteenth Amendment (1868) prevented the states from violating the "privileges and immunities" of its citizens or denying them "life, liberty, or property, without due process of law.'' The Fifteenth Amendment (1870) gave African-American men the right to vote.

The Fourteenth Amendment

Of these three amendments, the Fourteenth Amendment is one of the most widely used in court cases. The amendment says that states cannot violate the ''privileges and immunities'' of their citizens or deny them ''life, liberty, or property, without due process of law.'' But what exactly do these statements mean? What are the ''privileges and immunities'' and liberties that the states cannot violate? Historians and legal scholars still debate this question.

Some argue that the ''privileges and immunities'' and liberties protected by the Fourteenth Amendment are the rights and liberties protected by the Bill of Rights. They often point to statements made by the authors of the Fourteenth Amendment that it was intended to apply the Bill of Rights to the states. The amendment's author, Representative John A. Bingham, stated:

> [T]he privileges and immunities of the citizens of the United States . . . are chiefly defined in the first eight amendments to the Constitution. . . . These eight articles . . . were never limitations upon the power of the States, until made so by the Fourteenth Amendment.

The chief sponsor of the amendment in the Senate was Senator Jacob Howard. He also claimed that it was intended to ''restrain the power of the States and compel them at all times to respect these great fundamental guarantees.''

Others argue that the Fourteenth Amendment was not meant to apply the Bill of Rights to the states. In their view, the amendment was meant only to protect African Americans from discrimination in the South. They claim that the Fourteenth Amendment does not keep the states from denying many of the protections of the Bill of Rights.

There is probably no way to find out exactly what the Fourteenth Amendment was intended to mean. Because of this the Supreme Court at different times has read the amendment to mean very different things. The Court at first decided that the amendment did not apply the Bill of Rights to the states. In the *Slaughterhouse* cases in 1873 the Court ruled that the "privileges and immunities" protected by the Fourteenth Amendment were only a few unimportant rights. In 1884 the Court claimed in *Hurtado* v. *California* that the liberties protected by the amendment did not include those protected by the Bill of Rights. Not until the 1920s would the Supreme Court begin to use the Fourteenth Amendment and the Bill of Rights to protect freedom of expression.

Freedom of Speech and the Right to Dissent: From 1900 to 1931

"The question in every case is whether the words used are used in such circumstances and are of such a nature as to create a clear and present danger that they will bring about the substantive evils that Congress has a right to prevent."
JUSTICE OLIVER WENDELL HOLMES, in *Schenck* v. *United States* (1919)

The first attempt to define the meaning of the First Amendment came at time of great turmoil in the United States. Before the Civil War the United States had been mainly a nation of farmers. But the end of the war in 1865 marked the beginning of a great change. Between 1865 and 1900 swift industrialization changed the nation. Large cities sprang up as people left farms and small towns to work in the new industries. The promise of jobs and a new life lured millions of immigrants from Europe.

The changes created by industrialization brought many problems. Workers were often forced into low-paying and unsafe jobs. Poor workers and their families were crowded into unhealthy slums. The differences between rich and poor grew wider. Many immigrants faced discrimination in their adopted country.

Associate Justice Oliver Wendell Holmes served on the Supreme Court from 1902 to 1932. He wrote the unanimous opinion in a 1919 case that set limits on government control of free speech. In cases in which the speech presented a "clear and present danger," free speech could be limited.

The first Labor Day parade in New York City, 1882. Workers marched around Union Square, a small park. The last decades of the nineteenth century and the first decades of the twentieth were marked by a growing labor movement and by protests.

These inequalities and injustices led many people to question the U.S. political and economic system. Most people tried to improve their lives through peaceful change. Some people took to radical ideas such as socialism. A few even called for the use of violence to overthrow the government.

Such ideas scared many Americans. Their fear was so great that they felt threatened by anyone who criticized the economic and political system of the United States. Even those who wanted peaceful change faced suppression. In 1909 a radical speaker was arrested for reading the Declaration of Independence aloud!

World War I (1914–18) raised the fears of dissent. Although the fighting never came close to our shores, the government passed many laws during the war that restricted the First Amendment. Laws forbade the use of "disloyal, profane, scurrilous, or abusive language'' about the government, the Constitution, the flag, or the military. During the war, the government set up the Committee on Public Information. This group encouraged people to spy on their neighbors to detect any disloyalty.

Many German Americans and opponents of the war faced arrest by the government or violence by people taking the law into their own hands. Police in Carmel, Illinois, arrested the Reverend Samuel Siebert for preaching an antiwar sermon. One newspaper headline exclaimed: ''NEAR LYNCHINGS GIVE PRO-GERMANS NEEDED LESSON.''

The "Red Scare"

The mood of fear and intolerance did not stop when the war ended in 1918. The Russian Revolution in 1917 brought a Communist government to power in that country. This event frightened many Americans into thinking that a Communist revolution was about to take place in the United States. During the ''Red Scare,'' from 1919 to 1921, a wave of fear swept across the United States. Police arrested thousands of persons as potential ''radicals'' and ''revolutionaries.''

Most people arrested during the ''Red Scare'' were guilty of nothing more than foreign birth, criticizing the United States, or bad luck. One man went to jail just for stating that Lenin, leader of the Communist revolution in Russia, was one of the ''brainiest'' of world leaders. Another man was arrested because he ''looked like a radical.'' The state of Washington forbade schoolteachers to answer their students' questions about communism.

The public's mood of fear and suspicion matched that of the government. Angry mobs attacked foreigners and striking union members, whom they considered to be Communists. A crowd cheered and applauded when an angry sailor shot a man for refusing to rise during the playing of ''The Star-Spangled Banner.''

A few people did speak out against the violations of liberty during the ''Red Scare.'' Several of these people formed the

American Civil Liberties Union (ACLU) in 1920 to fight for the rights of those arrested. But the *Washington Post* stated the view of most Americans when it wrote, "There is no time to waste hair-splitting over infringement of liberty."

It was in this period of turmoil that the Supreme Court first began to wrestle with the meaning of the First Amendment. Most of the Supreme Court justices shared the fears of the era. They worried that revolution might break out in the United States. This fear made the Court willing to ban any speech that criticized the United States. Most of the justices believed that such criticism *might* cause violence or harm, whether the speaker intended it or not. In the view of the Court, "the spark may kindle a fire that, smoldering for a time, may burst into a sweeping and destructive conflagration [terrible fire]."

The Supreme Court used this logic to find even the most peaceful voices of change guilty of stirring up disorder and revolution. In perhaps the most famous case of the period, the Supreme Court in 1919 upheld the conviction of Eugene Debs.

Debs was the leader of the Socialist party in the United States. Born in Indiana, he went to work on the railroad at the age of fifteen. The bad conditions faced by many workers shocked the young man. Debs became a union leader and a Socialist. He fought to improve the lives of poor workers. Debs hated violence. He wanted to bring about peaceful change within the political system. These views made Debs popular with many workers. As the Socialist party's presidential candidate in 1912, he received nearly a million votes.

Debs opposed the United States's entry into World War I. He was also against the denial of the rights of those who were viewed as "disloyal." In 1918 he said:

No wonder Johnson [Samuel Johnson, an English writer] said that "Patriotism is the last refuge of scoundrels." He had the Wall Street gentry in mind . . . for in every age it has been the tyrant who has wrapped himself in the cloak of patriotism, or religion, or both. . . .

The United States, under the rule of the plutocracy [rich], is the only country that would send a woman to the penitentiary for 10 years for exercising her constitutional right of free speech. If this be treason let them make the most of it. . . .

Do not worry, please; don't worry over the charges of Treason to your masters, but be concerned about the Treason that involves yourselves. Be true to yourself, and you cannot be a traitor to any cause on earth.

Debs was arrested for making this statement. A jury found him guilty of causing disloyalty in the military and sentenced him to ten years in prison. In 1919 the Supreme Court agreed with the conviction. Debs was finally pardoned by President Warren G. Harding in 1921.

"A Clear and Present Danger"

The Supreme Court's opinion in the *Debs* case was written by Oliver Wendell Holmes. Holmes believed that the First Amendment did not grant an absolute right to free speech and that certain types of speech can be forbidden. To find out what types of speech could be banned, Holmes proposed using the "clear and present danger" test. Holmes had presented this argument the day before in another important free speech and free press case—*Schenck* v. *United States* (1919). According to Holmes:

The question in every case is whether the words used are used in such circumstances and are of such a nature as to create a clear and present danger that they will bring about the substantive [real] evils that Congress has a right to prevent.

Justice Holmes developed the "clear and present danger" test with Justice Louis D. Brandeis. Justice Brandeis explained that a "clear and present danger" existed only when serious violence was "so imminent [likely to happen] that it may befall [occur] before there is opportunity for full discussion." If enough time

Police officers and clerks load a police ambulance with books, magazines, and pamphlets seized from a Communist organization in Cambridge, Massachusetts, in 1919. During the "Red Scare," the Supreme Court in *Schenck* v. *United States* (1919) upheld the conviction of a man for circulating antidraft leaflets among members of the armed forces.

existed to "expose through discussion the falsehood and fallacies [inaccuracies], to avert the evil by the process of education, the remedy to be applied is more speech, not enforced silence." Even if the danger is likely, said Holmes, "There must be probability of serious injury to the state."

To show his point, Holmes used the example of someone falsely shouting fire in a crowded theater. Such an action created a "clear and present danger," since it would cause panic and possible injuries before the truth could be known. The First Amendment did not protect this type of speech. By this reasoning, the First Amendment *would not* protect someone who told an angry mob to burn down an army base or throw a bomb at the White House. The

First Amendment, however, *would* protect someone who merely called for a revolution or opposition to the war.

Holmes believed that the speech given by Eugene Debs presented a "clear and present danger." He explained that the nation was at war and that this created special circumstances. During war, statements that might be allowed in peacetime could be restricted by the government. In the opinion of Holmes and the other members of the Court, Debs's speech might have harmed the war effort by leading young men to oppose the draft.

Although all the other members of the Supreme Court agreed with Holmes and Brandeis in the *Schenck* and *Debs* cases, they soon began to disagree about what types of speech were dangerous. This disagreement came out most strongly in the case of *Abrams* v. *United States* (1919), which the Court decided only a few months after the *Debs* case.

The *Abrams* case began in New York City in 1918 when a group of radicals were arrested for distributing "subversive" leaflets. The leaflets criticized the sending of U.S. troops to Russia to help enemies of the Communist government there. The leaflets also called for workers in weapons plants to go on strike to protest the U.S. intervention in Russia.

The Supreme Court ruled that the radicals had violated the Sedition Act. This law had been passed by Congress in 1918. The law made it a crime to incite, or stir up, revolution or to urge that weapons production for the war effort be slowed.

Justices Holmes and Brandeis had other ideas. They thought that the Court was going too far in placing limits on free speech. They said that the Court was forbidding certain types of speech not because they were dangerous, but because people didn't like them. In their view, such actions violated the ideals of the Constitution. In the case of *Abrams* v. *United States* (1919), Holmes wrote:

> I think that we should be eternally vigilant [always alert] against attempts to check the expression of opinions that we loathe and believe to be fraught with death, unless they so imminently threaten

immediate interference with the lawful and pressing purposes of the law that an immediate check is required to save the country.

The clash of views between Holmes and Brandeis on the one hand and the rest of the Court on the other in the *Abrams* case reflects a basic debate over democracy. Most members of the Court in the 1920s held a very limited view of the ability of the American people for democracy. They believed that ordinary people could not decide which ideas were true and which were false, which ideas were dangerous and which were helpful. Because of the public's ignorance, the Court believed it was necessary for the government to decide what the people should hear, speak, and think.

Unlike the other members of the Court, Holmes and Brandeis were more positive about the wisdom of the American people. They believed that over time the people would make the right choices for the country. They argued that history has shown democracies to make many mistakes. But, in the view of Holmes and Brandeis, the honest mistakes of a free people are surely better than the willing abuses of tyrants and dictators.

The "Incorporation" of Free Speech

As the 1920s wore on, both the nation and the Court retreated from the fear and panic of World War I and the "Red Scare." Most people came to realize that a Communist revolution in the United States was not just around the corner and that the nation had overreacted in its attempts to forbid "dangerous" speech. This change of thought gradually caused the Court to favor the views of Holmes and Brandeis and to expand the protection of the First Amendment.

The first sign of the Supreme Court's new attitude came in the 1925 case of *Gitlow* v. *New York*. Here the Court ruled for the first time that the guarantee of liberty in the Fourteenth Amendment required states to protect freedom of speech. The case involved Benjamin Gitlow, a radical Socialist. Gitlow published a pamphlet with the title *Left Wing Manifesto*. The pamphlet called for the overthrow of the U.S. government and replacing it with a "Communist state."

The police arrested Gitlow for violating New York's law against advocating the overthrow of the U.S. government by violence "or by any unlawful means." Gitlow appealed his arrest. He claimed that New York's law violated his right to free speech and press. Gitlow argued that the Fourteenth Amendment meant that the states as well as the federal government could not restrict his right to free speech under the First Amendment.

The Court upheld Gitlow's conviction. But it agreed with his claim that the Fourteenth Amendment kept states from limiting freedom of speech. According to Justice Edward T. Sanford:

> For present purposes we may and do assume that freedom of speech and of the press—which are protected by the First Amendment from abridgement by Congress—are among the fundamental personal rights and "liberties" protected by the due process clause of the Fourteenth Amendment from impairment by the States.

No one is sure why the Supreme Court decided to do this. More important is the fact that the Supreme Court now viewed freedom of speech and press to be two of the liberties protected by the due process clause of the Fourteenth Amendment. This section of the Fourteenth Amendment says that states could not deprive "any person of life, liberty, or property, without due process of law." In legal terms, the Court had "incorporated" part of the First Amendment into the Fourteenth Amendment.

The Court restated its view in the 1931 case of *Near* v. *Minnesota*. Chief Justice Charles Evans Hughes wrote the opinion of the Court. He stated:

> It is no longer open to doubt that the liberty of the press and of speech is within the liberty safeguarded by the due process clause of the Fourteenth Amendment. It was found impossible to conclude that this essential liberty of the citizen was left unprotected by the general guaranty of fundamental rights of person and property.

Benjamin Gitlow (right), vice-presidential candidate of the Workers party, at a rally in Madison Square Garden in New York City, 1928. In *Gitlow* v. *New York* (1925), the Supreme Court upheld a state law that made it a crime to call for the overthrow of the government by force. But the Court ruled that freedom of the press and speech are protected from actions by the states.

The decisions in the *Gitlow* and *Near* cases led the way for the Supreme Court to "incorporate" the other parts of the First Amendment into the Fourteenth Amendment. In 1937, in *DeJonge* v. *Oregon,* the Court included freedom of assembly in the rights protected from state law. The Court in *Cantwell* v. *Connecticut* (1940) and *Everson* v. *Board of Education* (1947) said that states could not violate the First Amendment's guarantee of the people's right to religious freedom.

These decisions meant that the Supreme Court now believed that Congress *and* the states could make no law abridging the freedoms of speech, press, religion, and public assembly. The application of the First Amendment to the states marked an important advance for freedom of expression.

The Supreme Court Looks Closely at Free Speech

In 1931, the Supreme Court finally struck down a law that violated freedom of speech. It happened in the case of *Stromberg* v.

California. As a teenager in the 1920s, Yetta Stromberg worked in a camp for the children of political radicals. The camp taught that capitalism (the economic system in the United States) was evil. It also taught about the need for workers to join together to overthrow that system. At the camp Stromberg and the children faced the red flag of the Communist party and pledged allegiance "to the worker's red flag, and to the cause for which it stands; one aim throughout our lives, freedom for the working class." Yetta was arrested for breaking California's law against showing the Communist flag.

Yetta appealed her case to the U.S. Supreme Court. In 1931 the Court ruled that Yetta was innocent. Chief Justice Charles Evans Hughes wrote that the California law was unconstitutional since it banned even the most peaceful forms of free speech. Just pledging allegiance to a red flag did not create a serious or immediate danger that would justify restricting a person's right to free speech.

The *Stromberg* case showed that the Supreme Court was beginning to look closely at any law that restricted free speech. The Court was no longer willing to let states alone decide which types of speech were allowed and which were not. Vaguely worded laws that restricted peaceful and orderly forms of speech as well as dangerous and violent ones would be ruled unconstitutional.

The Court justified its view because it held free speech to be necessary to a democratic society. Without free speech, the other freedoms granted in the Constitution and Bill of Rights had no meaning. Now, any time the government wanted to limit the people's right to free speech, it would have to prove that there was some very important reason to do so.

As a result of this doctrine the Court in the 1930s and 1940s began to rule that many laws restricting free speech were unconstitutional. This meant that American citizens now had greater protection for the right to oppose peacefully the actions of the government. This is one of the most important rights of a free people.

Freedom of Speech
and the Right to Dissent:
From the Cold War to the 1960s

"[O]verthrow of the Government by force and violence is certainly a substantial enough interest for the Government to limit speech."

CHIEF JUSTICE FRED M. VINSON,
in *Dennis et al.* v. *United States* (1951)

"To the Founders of this Nation, the benefits derived from free expression were worth the risks."

JUSTICE HUGO L. BLACK,
in *Dennis et al.* v. *United States* (1951)

Although the nation faced a much greater danger in World War II (1939–45) than in World War I, the United States did not experience the widespread abuse of free speech that took place during the previous war. The end of World War II did bring a return of anti-Communist fears, however.

During most of World War II the United States and the Soviet Union were allies in the fight against Nazi Germany and Japan. Unfortunately, the U.S.–Soviet friendship did not continue after the war ended in 1945. The Soviet takeover of Eastern Europe after the war led many Americans to believe that Stalin, leader of the Soviet Union, was trying to rule the world just as Hitler had tried to. In the postwar years, a "cold war" broke out between the United States and the Soviet Union. During this time, tensions ran high as each country tried to dominate the other without going to war.

Associate Justice William O. Douglas served on the Supreme Court from 1939 to 1975. He was one of the strongest supporters of First Amendment rights, especially the right to freedom of speech.

Just as in the 1920s, many Americans in the postwar years believed that Communists within the United States were trying to overthrow the government. People believed that Communists had made their way into important jobs in the nation's unions, churches, movie industry, and government. To root out the influence of Communists and their ideas, the government investigated "un-American activities." It forced its employees to take loyalty oaths and passed several laws restricting the activities of the Communist party. Anyone thought to be a Communist was forbidden to join a union. Schools and libraries removed books believed to support Communist ideas. People were accused of Communist connections if they had friends or relatives who were believed to be Communists.

While these investigations did discover some true Communists, a widespread Communist plot existed only in the minds of some overly fearful Americans. Their fear often led them to overreact. For example, the state of Indiana considered banning *Robin Hood* from school libraries because its hero robbed the rich and gave to the poor—an action that some considered communistic.

Worse still were the false accusations that came from "witch-hunting" campaigns. These campaigns were attempts to find Communists in various organizations. The accusations that resulted ruined the lives and careers of many loyal Americans. In one case, the U.S. Air Force listed a soldier as a possible Communist because his father, a Yugoslavian immigrant, had been reading newspapers from his Communist-ruled homeland. Several American actors, playwrights, and movie directors could not find work because they were considered Communists. The chief bishop of the Methodist church was even accused of having Communist associations.

Senator Joseph McCarthy of Wisconsin was the leader of the anti-Communist crusade. During the early 1950s, McCarthy made many reckless accusations against innocent people. His actions added a new word to the dictionary—*McCarthyism*. This word has come to mean any false attempt to destroy a person's reputation.

The actions of McCarthy and his supporters had a chilling effect on free speech. Many people worried that they would be labeled as

Senator Joseph McCarthy at the Senate-Army hearings in 1954. When the senator accused army officials and other respected government officials of Communist sympathies, the public finally turned against him.

Communists if they made any comments critical of the United States or capitalism. Others declined to join liberal political organizations for fear that they might be seen as members of "subversive" organizations.

Freedom of Speech During the Cold War

The cold war led to another argument over the people's right to free speech versus the country's need for national security. Some believed the threat posed by communism was so great that free speech had to be restricted or else the country would be placed in danger. Others believed that the danger of communism was not as great as the danger posed by limiting free speech.

The debate over free speech reached the U.S. Supreme Court in 1951 in the case of *Dennis et al.* v. *United States*. The FBI arrested Eugene Dennis and ten other Communist party leaders in 1947 for violating the Smith Act. The Smith Act was passed in 1940. The act made it a crime to organize a Communist party or call for the forceful overthrow of the government. It became a crime to merely *plan* to do these things.

The *Dennis* case showed the Court's willingness to sacrifice the right of free speech for national security. The Court's majority ruled that the threat posed by Communists was so great that it justified restricting the people's freedom of speech. The Court took this stand even if it was unlikely that the actions of Dennis and his associates would ever lead to violence. In the words of Chief Justice Fred Vinson, the author of the Court's opinion in the *Dennis* case, the government need not "wait until the *putsch* [revolt] is about to be executed, the plans have been laid and the signal is awaited" before it limits free speech.

The Court's opinion in *Dennis et al.* v. *United States* (1951) set back the people's right to free speech. Now, all the government needed to limit free speech was a *potential* danger, not, as in Justice Holmes's phrase, a "clear and present danger." The Supreme Court now understood the First Amendment to mean that *merely talking about or planning to talk about* falsely shouting fire in a crowded theater was illegal.

In balancing the people's right to free speech and the country's need for national security, the Court had clearly given greater weight to the country's need for national security. The cost was denying free speech to many loyal Americans. Even those who supported restricting free speech acknowledged this fact. Justice Felix Frankfurter stated, "Suppressing [putting down] advocates of overthrow inevitably will also silence critics who do not advocate overthrow but fear that their criticism may be so construed [understood]."

Like Justices Holmes and Brandeis thirty years before, Justices Hugo Black and William O. Douglas opposed the opinion of the rest of the Court in *Dennis et al.* v. *United States* (1951). In fact, Douglas had replaced Brandeis in 1939. Justice Black, who always carried a copy of the Constitution in his pocket, used a very strict interpretation of the First Amendment. For him, when the amendment said "Congress shall make no law," it meant "Congress shall make *no* law." Black thought *any* attempt to restrict the people's right to free speech was clearly a violation of the Constitution.

Justice Hugo Black understood that the spread of Communist ideas could be dangerous. But, he wrote, "To the Founders of this Nation, the benefits derived from free expression were worth the risks." He stated his hope that in the future, when the "pressures, passions, and fears" of the cold war had lessened, the Court would return to a correct interpretation of the First Amendment.

Justice William O. Douglas also believed that the Court was overreacting because of its fear of communism. For Douglas, the Communist ideas of Dennis and his associates had no appeal to most Americans. He believed that free speech offered the best defense against communism. Douglas wrote:

> Communism has been so thoroughly exposed in this country that it has been crippled as a political force. Free speech has destroyed it as an effective political party. . . . The country is not in despair; the people know Soviet Communism; the doctrine of Soviet revolution is exposed in all its ugliness and the American people want none of it.

Douglas's opinion points to another debate about free speech in a democracy. Many people, including most of the justices on the Supreme Court in the early 1950s, believed that freedom of speech is a weakness, not a strength. For them, freedom of speech creates the potential for dangerous ideas to infect the people, just as a virus might attack a body. The role of the government is therefore to act like a doctor. It has to prevent the spread of the disease of evil thoughts. Therefore, the government must say what is good and what is evil.

Others, like Black and Douglas, put more trust in the ability of the people to make correct choices. They believed that free speech is the best defense against dangerous ideas. In their view, if the people know all the facts and have a chance to think about a variety of ideas, then they will have the wisdom to make the right choices.

In the view of Black and Douglas, the "cure" of restricting free speech was worse than the "disease" of dangerous ideas. They believed it was self-defeating to take away the people's right to free speech, the foundation of democracy, to prevent an undemocratic government. Justice Douglas stated this best in 1951:

> In days of great tension when feelings run high, it is a temptation to take shortcuts by borrowing from the totalitarian techniques of our opponents. But when we do, we set in motion a subversive influence of our own design that destroys us from within.

A More Tolerant View of Free Speech

In time, the Supreme Court came to hold a more open view of free speech. This resulted in part from a lessening of cold war tensions. Also, in the United States fear of communism declined in the late 1950s. Another important factor was the appointment of Earl Warren as chief justice of the United States in 1953. As California's attorney general during World War II, Warren had helped to carry out the imprisonment of Japanese Americans. But as chief justice of the United States, Warren led a legal "revolution." During this time, the Supreme Court expanded the civil rights and liberties of many Americans. Warren's achievements on the Court earned him the nickname "Super Chief."

The Warren Court began to broaden the people's right to free speech. In *Yates* v. *United States* (1957) several members of California's Communist party who had been convicted for violating the Smith Act appealed their case to the Supreme Court. The Court reversed these convictions. It ruled that the government could no longer restrict speech that merely voiced a general idea of violence against the government. An example of this type of speech would be, "I think the government should be overthrown." From now on, the government could only restrict speech that voiced violence against the government. An example of this type of speech would be, "Go out today with guns and overthrow the government."

Though the Court's decision expanded freedom of speech, it did not satisfy Justices Black and Douglas. They continued to insist that the government lacked the right to forbid any type of speech. Black said, "I believe that the First Amendment forbids Congress to punish people for talking about public affairs, whether or not such discussion incites [leads] to action, legal or illegal."

The Supreme Court came closer to Black's position in the case of *Brandenburg* v. *Ohio* (1969). Clarence Brandenburg was a member of the Ohio Ku Klux Klan. He was convicted of calling for violence against the government at a Klan meeting in 1969. News films of the meeting showed hooded Klan members carrying guns, burning a cross, and muttering about "burning the niggers" and "sending the Jews back to Israel." Brandenburg gave a speech saying, "We're not a revengent [revengeful] organization, but if our President, our Congress, our Supreme Court, continues to suppress the white, Caucasian race, it's possible that there might have to be some revengeance [revenge] taken."

The Court voted to overrule Brandenburg's conviction. It struck down the Ohio law that had been used to convict him. The Court declared that the First Amendment did not allow laws "to forbid or proscribe [outlaw] advocacy of the use of force or of law violation except where such advocacy is directed to inciting or producing imminent [immediate] lawless action and is likely to incite or produce such action."

With the decision in the *Brandenburg* case, the Court had finally and firmly come to agree with the conclusion stated by Justices Holmes and Brandeis fifty years earlier: the only speech forbidden by the First Amendment is speech that offers a "clear and present danger." The decision in the *Brandenburg* case reaffirmed the belief of the Framers, the writers of the Constitution: in a democracy the people, not the government, have the wisdom and the right to decide which ideas are right and which are wrong.

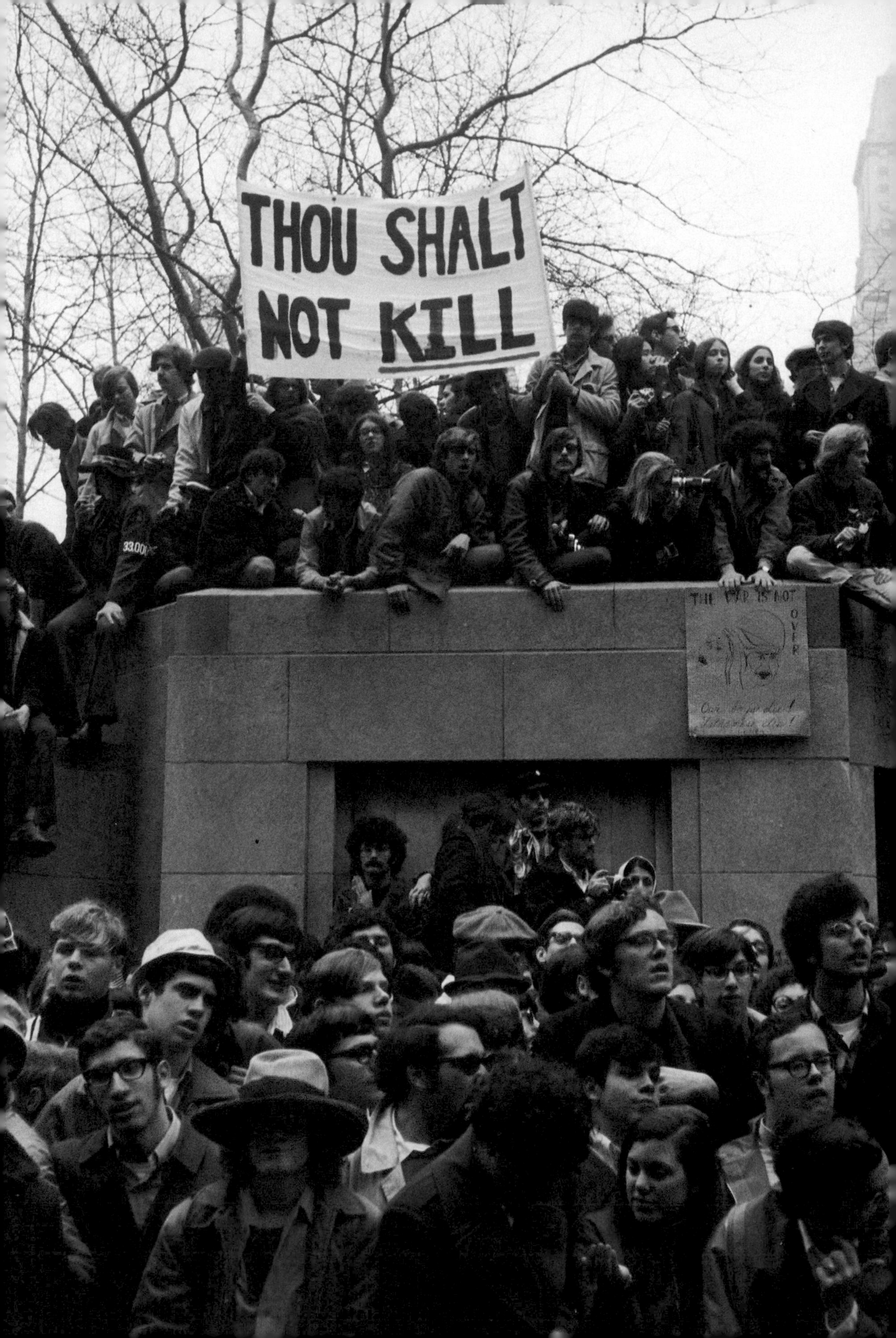
THOU SHALT
NOT KILL

Freedom of Speech: Symbolic Speech and "Fighting Words"

> "A function of free speech under our system of government is to invite dispute."
>
> JUSTICE WILLIAM O. DOUGLAS, in *Terminiello* v. *Chicago* (1949)

At the 1984 Republican National Convention in Dallas, Texas, thousands of Republicans cheered the renomination of President Ronald Reagan as the leader of their party. These Republicans and millions of other Americans believed President Reagan had brought back pride and prosperity to the United States. The convention delegates showed their enthusiasm and patriotism by waving hundreds of American flags.

Outside the convention hall were many protesters with a very different view of the United States. They saw millions in poverty, minorities who still faced discrimination, and bloody wars in Central America. Whereas the delegates inside the convention hall viewed the flag as a symbol of pride, many protesters outside saw it as a symbol of injustice. One of these protesters, Gregory Lee Johnson, even went so far as to burn the American flag.

Gregory Johnson's act that day in August 1984 became an important national issue. The years 1989 and 1990 saw a national debate about the right to burn the flag. This debate centered on two controversies about the limits of free speech—symbolic speech and "fighting words."

During the late 1960s and early 1970s, hundreds of thousands of people assembled to protest United States involvement in the war in Vietnam. Supporters of the war often called the antiwar protesters traitors.

Symbolic Speech

The First Amendment guarantees the right of free speech. But there are many forms of speech. The most recognizable form is pure speech. Pure speech is the use of the spoken word to convey a particular idea. Another form is symbolic speech. This refers to the use of symbolic objects or actions to express an idea. Examples of symbolic speech might be waving a flag or burning a cross.

The First Amendment protects nearly all forms of pure speech. It also protects many types of symbolic speech, like wearing a campaign button during an election or carrying a sign at a protest. However, the First Amendment does *not* protect all actions that have symbolic meaning. For example, beating your neighbor might be considered a symbolic way of expressing your dislike of that person. Yet such symbolic activities are obviously not protected by the First Amendment.

But which forms of symbolic actions does the First Amendment protect? For example, many people believe that the First Amendment protected Gregory Johnson. They argue that burning the American flag is a symbolic action meant to express political views. Others believe that the First Amendment does *not* protect a person's right to burn the flag. These people claim that burning the flag is more action than speech.

The Supreme Court Looks at Symbolic Speech

The Supreme Court began to address the question of symbolic speech in the 1930s. In *Stromberg* v. *California* (1931), the Supreme Court ruled that a California law against showing a red flag was unconstitutional. (See Chapter 4.) The 1930s also saw the Court uphold the right of striking workers to picket their places of work. Their picketing often consisted of demonstrating in front of their work places with signs of protest. The Court viewed picketing as a symbolic exercise of free speech.

Another test of symbolic speech came during the civil rights movement. The civil rights movement began in the 1950s when African Americans began to protest racial discrimination and the denial of their rights as American citizens. Many in the movement used peaceful forms of protest, such as boycotts, demonstrations, and sit-ins.

In 1960, African-American students staged sit-ins in restaurants that refused to serve black customers. They sat quietly and peacefully in the restaurants to protest discrimination against blacks. Many protesters suffered insults and physical beatings because of their actions. Many were arrested.

In 1961 the Supreme Court upheld the right of the protesters to stage sit-ins. Justice John Marshall Harlan wrote that a sit-in was as much a form of expression as the spoken word:

It, like speech, appeals to good sense and to "the power of reason as applied through public discussion" . . . just as much, if not more than, a public oration [speech] delivered from a soapbox at a street corner. This Court has never limited the right to speak . . . to mere verbal expression.

Throughout the 1960s the Supreme Court expanded the First Amendment to include many types of symbolic speech. One of the most important cases involving symbolic speech at this time was *Tinker* v. *Des Moines Independent Community School District* (1969).

In December 1965, Mary Beth Tinker was an eighth-grade junior high school student in Des Moines, Iowa. At that time, the United States was increasing the number of American troops being sent to fight in the Vietnam War. Mary Beth and her family opposed the war. They believed that the United States should try to settle the dispute peacefully. Mary Beth and her friend Christopher (Chris) Eckhardt decided to wear black armbands to school to show their opposition to the war.

Just after lunch, Mary Beth was called into the school principal's office. The principal, Chester Pratt, told her that her armband was against school policy. He said it might be "disruptive," although no disruptions had taken place. Mary Beth agreed to take off her armband, but Pratt suspended her from school for one week anyway. Chris Eckhardt was also suspended from his high school. The next day Mary Beth's older brother John also received a suspension from his high school for wearing an armband.

Mary Beth's actions created a storm of controversy in Des Moines. Many felt that opposing the war was equal to treason. People called Mary Beth and her family Communists and splashed red paint on their house. The Tinkers received many threats. Some people even threatened to kill them.

Mary Beth Tinker with her mother and her younger brother. She had worn the black armband to school to protest the Vietnam War. The Des Moines, Iowa, school she attended had tried to prevent her from exercising her right to freedom of speech. In 1969, the Supreme Court ruled in Tinker's favor.

But the Tinkers were not afraid. They believed that the suspension was unfair, and they decided to go to court to have it reversed. They argued that the school had violated Mary Beth's constitutional right to free speech.

The case of *Tinker* v. *Des Moines Independent Community School District* came before the Supreme Court. In 1969, the Court decided by a vote of 7 to 2 that Mary Beth was right. Justice Abe Fortas gave the opinion of the Court. He wrote that students did not "shed their constitutional rights to freedom of expression at the schoolhouse gate." The Court ruled that Mary Beth's armband was a legal form of symbolic speech.

The flag is one of the most important symbols of the United States. One's attitude toward the flag usually represents one's attitude toward the United States. For example, people often use the term *flag-waver* to refer to someone who is very patriotic. On the other hand, when someone is extremely critical or abusive about the United States, they are considered to be "trampling on the flag."

During the civil rights movement of the 1960s and the Vietnam War, many people used the flag to express their protests. In 1966 Sidney Street burned an American flag to protest the shooting of James Meredith, a civil rights worker. As the flag burned, Street said, "If they did that to Meredith, we don't need an American flag."

Another incident involving the flag occurred in 1970. That year a young man named Spence, outraged over the killing of four student protesters at Kent State University, put a peace symbol on the American flag and flew it from his apartment window. Spence said, "I felt there had been so much killing and that this is not what America stood for. I felt that the flag stood for America and I wanted people to know that I thought America stood for peace."

In both cases the police arrested the protesters for mistreating the flag. And in both cases the Supreme Court overruled their convictions. The Court held that both persons had been symbolically exercising their right to free speech.

The Controversy Over
Gregory Johnson's Flag Burning

These cases set the stage for the controversy over Gregory Johnson's burning of the flag outside the 1984 Republican National Convention. The police arrested Johnson for violating a Texas law against destroying the American flag. The case finally reached the Supreme Court in 1989. The issue of flag burning strongly divided the justices. Five justices voted to overturn Johnson's conviction, and four voted to uphold it. The reason given was that the Texas law violated the First Amendment.

The Court's minority argued that the flag had a special place as our national symbol and should be protected. Justice John Paul Stevens wrote that the flag is a symbol "of freedom, of equal opportunity, or religious tolerance and of good will for other peoples who share our aspirations [goals]." Since many Americans had fought and died for these ideals, "it cannot be true that the flag that uniquely symbolizes their power is not itself worthy of protection from unnecessary desecration [insult]."

Chief Justice William Rehnquist also opposed protecting the right to burn the flag. He believed that flag burning was not a form of symbolic speech. According to Rehnquist, ". . . [F]lag burning is the equivalent of an inarticulate [dumb] grunt or roar that, it seems fair to say, is most likely to be indulged in not to express any particular idea, but to antagonize [anger] others."

Most of the Court argued otherwise. Justice William Brennan wrote the majority opinion. He stated his belief that although many people found flag burning to be offensive this was no reason to forbid it. He wrote, "If there is a bedrock [basic] principle underlying the First Amendment, it is that the Government may not prohibit the expression of an idea simply because society finds the idea itself offensive or disagreeable."

Justice Brennan went on to say that by protecting Gregory Johnson's right to free speech, the role of the flag would be strengthened. According to Brennan, "The way to preserve the

Gregory Johnson's conviction for burning an American flag was overturned by the Supreme Court. In *Texas* v. *Johnson* (1989), the Court ruled that the First Amendment protects a person's right to burn the U.S. flag as a symbolic action. Two of the Court's most conservative members, Justices Antonin Scalia and Anthony Kennedy, were among the majority to vote for this decision. The Court ruling was a very controversial one.

flag's special role is not to punish those who feel differently about these matters. It is to persuade them that they are wrong.''

The Court's decision in *Texas* v. *Johnson* (1989) set off a controversy. Many people opposed the view of the Court. They believed that the flag was an important national symbol and should be protected. Veterans groups saw the decision as an insult to American soldiers who had fought and died for the flag.

President George Bush immediately spoke out against the decision. He said, ''Flag burning is wrong—dead wrong.'' Bush, along with most Republicans and some Democrats, wanted to overrule the Court by adding an amendment to the Constitution that would make flag burning against the law.

Many Democrats in Congress also disagreed with the Court. But they were against changing the Constitution. Fearful that doing nothing about flag burning would make them unpopular with the voters, they wrote a *federal* law against flag burning. They hoped that the Court would approve the new federal law. But they hoped in vain.

In a new case, the Supreme Court struck down the federal law against flag burning in June 1990. Again President Bush and others called for an amendment to the Constitution. But many members of Congress would not support changing the Constitution to limit the First Amendment. The amendment against flag burning fell short of getting the needed two-thirds of the votes in the House and the Senate as a step toward becoming an amendment. The amendment's failure ended much of the controversy over flag burning. But the controversy over the limits of symbolic speech will certainly go on.

"Fighting Words"

Gregory Johnson's burning of the flag in 1984 also represents an example of ''fighting words.'' ''Fighting words'' refers to types of speech that listeners find deeply offensive and against which they are likely to react violently. Many people honor the flag. The sight of someone burning it might lead them to violence against the flag burners. Religious slurs, racist and sexist comments, and personal insults are other examples of "fighting words."

Does the First Amendment protect the people's right to use "fighting words"? Some argue that it does not. They claim that nothing in the amendment gives people the right to insult, to abuse verbally, or to harass others.

Other people argue that speech cannot be forbidden just because certain people might find it offensive. They claim that banning such speech amounts to a "hecklers' veto." A "hecklers' veto" refers to the idea that people opposed to any type of speech could effectively forbid it by acting violently against its speaker. In these instances, strong supporters of the First Amendment argue, the law should restrict those who become violent, not those who merely speak.

The Supreme Court and "Fighting Words"

The first important case to deal with the issue of "fighting words" involved a Jehovah's Witness named Chaplinsky. In 1942 Chaplinsky stood on a street in Rochester, New Hampshire. He was passing out religious literature. But he was also calling all other religions "rackets." Chaplinsky's statements soon drew an angry crowd. The police soon arrived and arrested him. On the way to the police station Chaplinsky called the city marshal a "racketeer and a damned Fascist." He claimed that Fascists ran the city of Rochester. At that time the United States was at war with the forces of Nazi Germany and Fascist Italy.

A jury convicted Chaplinsky of violating the New Hampshire law against offensive speech. The Supreme Court upheld the verdict. Justice Robert H. Jackson wrote that the First Amendment did not protect the "fighting words" uttered by Chaplinsky. In Justice Jackson's view, "fighting words" are "no essential part of any exposition [statement] of ideas, and are of such slight social value as a step to truth that any benefit that may be derived from them is clearly outweighed by the social interest in order and morality."

Since the decision in the *Chaplinsky* case, the Supreme Court has continued to place "fighting words" outside the protection of the First Amendment. The Court, however, has narrowed greatly the types of speech that it considers "fighting words." One case involved Father Arthur Terminiello, a Roman Catholic priest who gave a speech full of racist and anti-Semitic statements in 1946. The speech caused an angry mob to gather outside the hall in Chicago where the priest was speaking. He called those in the crowd "snakes" and "slimy scum." The mob beat up those who tried to get inside. Father Terminiello was found guilty of disorderly conduct and fined.

The Supreme Court voted to overturn Father Terminiello's conviction in 1949. Justice William O. Douglas gave the opinion of the Court. He said that Terminiello's speech caused "dispute" and "anger" but did not offer a "clear and present danger." Douglas wrote:

A function of free speech under our system of government is to invite dispute. It may indeed best serve its high purposes when it induces [causes] a condition of unrest, creates dissatisfaction with conditions the way they are, or even stirs people to anger. Speech is often provocative and challenging. It may strike at prejudices and preconceptions and have profound unsettling effects as it presses for acceptance of an idea.

The Skokie Dispute

Perhaps the most famous case of "fighting words" took place in 1977. The case concerned the First Amendment rights of the American Nazis. That spring a group of American Nazis based in Chicago announced their intention to march in the nearby suburb of Skokie. Of Skokie's 70,000 residents at the time, 40,500 were Jews, and about 7,000 were survivors of Hitler's death camps where millions of Jews had been routinely murdered. Many of Skokie's families had lost members to the Nazi gas chambers of Auschwitz and Treblinka.

The thought of Nazis marching in their community brought back terrible memories to many of Skokie's residents. They believed that they owed it to the Holocaust victims and to the world to stop the Nazis. Their cry was "Never again!"

Many others, Jews and non-Jews, echoed these feelings. They believed that the Nazis must be stopped. Thousands planned to attend counterdemonstrations. The fear of bloodshed grew.

The feelings of the community and the fear of violence forced the Skokie village council to take action. They passed ordinances, local laws, that banned the handing out of materials that would arouse racial or religious hatred. They then obtained a court order stopping the Nazis' march. The Skokie council argued that the presence of the Nazis and of their symbol, the swastika, were in fact "fighting words." These images were so offensive to the townspeople that their very sight would provoke violence.

American Nazi leader Frank Collin. Federal courts supported the right of American Nazis to hold a march through Skokie, Illinois, a suburb of Chicago with a large Jewish population.

The American Civil Liberties Union (ACLU) represented the Nazis in court. The ACLU has fought for First Amendment issues since the 1920s. Its decision to defend the Nazis caused thousands of ACLU members to resign. They argued that defenders of free speech had no business helping Nazis who wanted to deny that right to others.

Aryeh Neier, the ACLU's executive director, defended the group's decision.

> As a Jew, and a refugee from Nazi Germany, I have strong personal reasons for finding Nazis repugnant [disgusting]. Freedom of speech protects my right to denounce the Nazis with all the vehemence [deep feeling and strength] I think proper. Despite my hatred of their vicious doctrine, I realize that it is in my interests to defend their right to preach it.

Neier and others claimed that the First Amendment protected anyone, including Nazis, or it protected no one. The ACLU argued that the same reasons for stopping the Nazis could be used to prevent other, peaceful groups from demonstrating. It viewed the threats of violence against the march as a "hecklers' veto." According to the ACLU, the law should restrain the hostile audience and not the speaker.

With these arguments, the two sides went to court. After a series of legal battles, the case went to the Illinois Supreme Court. The court voted 6 to 1 to let the Nazis march and to display the swastika. They ruled that the First Amendment protected displaying the swastika as a form of symbolic speech. The court acknowledged the trauma the swastika caused for many in Skokie. And it knew that violence might result from the march. Yet the court refused to forbid the march. In the words of the court, "a hostile audience is not a basis for restraining otherwise legal First Amendment activity."

The case then went to the federal district court in 1978. District Court Judge Bernard Decker agreed with the decision of the Illinois

Supreme Court. Decker wrote that Skokie could not restrict the Nazis' right to express their philosophy, "however obnoxious . . . that philosophy may be." According to Judge Decker:

> [I]t is better to allow those who preach racial hate to expend [use] their venom in rhetoric [words] rather than [for us to be] panicked into embarking on the dangerous course of permitting the government to decide what its citizens may say and hear. . . . The ability of American society to tolerate the advocacy even of the hateful doctrines espoused [put forth] by the plaintiffs without abandoning its commitment to freedom of speech and assembly is perhaps the best protection we have against the establishment of any Nazi-type regime in this country.

Judge Decker's decision was upheld by the U.S. court of appeals. The appeals court stated that if First Amendment rights "are to remain vital for all, they must protect not only those society deems [regards as] acceptable, but also those whose ideas it quite justifiably rejects and despises." In October 1978 the U.S. Supreme Court refused to hear the case. By then the Nazis had agreed not to march in Skokie in exchange for the right to march in Chicago.

The examples of Gregory Lee Johnson and the Illinois Nazis show that upholding the people's right to free speech is not easy. Doing so requires us to tolerate people and ideas that we might consider hateful and perhaps even dangerous. The Framers knew this when they wrote the First Amendment. But still they went ahead. They had faith in the people and their institutions to meet this great challenge.

Freedom of Religion: "Establishment of Religion"

"I contemplate with solemn reverence that act of the American people [the First Amendment] which declared that their legislature should 'make no law respecting an establishment of religion or prohibiting the free exercise thereof,' thus building a wall of separation between church and state."

THOMAS JEFFERSON, 1802

The First Amendment to the Constitution states, "Congress shall make no law respecting an establishment of religion, or prohibiting the free exercise thereof." The Framers of the amendment must have considered this very important since they placed it at the beginning. They knew that religious intolerance caused most violations of free expression in England and colonial America. As Justice Hugo Black wrote:

Catholics found themselves hounded and proscribed [condemned] because of their faith; Quakers who followed their conscience went to jail; Baptists were peculiarly obnoxious to certain dominant Protestant sects; men and women of varied faiths who happened to be in a minority in a particular locality were persecuted because they steadfastly persisted [continued] in worshipping God only as their own consciences dictated. And all of these dissenters were compelled to pay tithes [income paid to a church] and taxes to support government-sponsored churches whose ministers preached inflammatory sermons designed to strengthen and consolidate the

A New England church. Freedom of religion has attracted millions of immigrants to the United States over the past three and a half centuries.

established faith by generating a burning hatred against dissenters.

These practices became so commonplace as to shock the freedom-loving colonials into a feeling of abhorrence [disgust]. . . . It was these feelings which found expression in the First Amendment.

To protect against future acts of intolerance, the founders of our nation called, in the First Amendment, for the separation of church and state. In 1802, Thomas Jefferson wrote in a letter to the Baptists of Danbury, Connecticut, that the amendment built ''a wall of separation between church and state.'' James Madison echoed this thought thirty years later when he spoke of a ''line of separation'' between religion and government.

What do the phrases ''wall of separation,'' ''line of separation,'' ''establishment of religion,'' and ''free exercise'' mean? The exact aims of the Framers are unknown, but this much seems clear. They wanted to make sure that the federal government did nothing to encourage or support one church or religious belief. They also wanted to prevent any laws that kept people from worshipping as they wished.

The Supreme Court and ''Establishment of Religion''

Establishment of religion concerns active government support of religion, especially support of a specific religion. By the mid-1800s, most states had done away with direct support for any one religion. Many states still gave indirect support to religions, however. One example of this was including religious instruction in public schools. Not until the 1940s did the Supreme Court begin to build ''a wall of separation between church and state.''

The first important case in this area was *Everson* v. *Board of Education* (1947). The case dealt with a New Jersey law that authorized school districts to arrange for the transport of students to their schools. A New Jersey town, acting under the law, paid the bus fares of students who went to Roman Catholic schools. Some people complained that the law violated the First Amendment by helping to support Roman Catholic schools, an establishment of religion.

Until the *Everson* case the First Amendment prevented only the federal government from passing laws "respecting an establishment of religion." Since *the state* of New Jersey had passed the law about how it was going to spend tax money (a state's right), the First Amendment did not seem to apply. But the Supreme Court, beginning in the 1920s, had begun to rule that the liberties protected from interference by the states in the Fourteenth Amendment included many of the rights mentioned in the First Amendment. (See Chapter 5.)

In the *Everson* case the Supreme Court ruled for the first time that the Fourteenth Amendment prevented the states, as well as the federal government, from passing laws "respecting an establishment of religion." In legal terms, the Supreme Court had "incorporated" the First Amendment's establishment clause into the Fourteenth Amendment. Justice Hugo Black wrote that this meant:

> Neither a state nor the Federal Government can set up a church. Neither can pass laws which aid one religion, aid all religions, or prefer one religion over another. . . . No tax in any amount, large or small, can be levied to support any religious activity or institutions, whatever they may be called, or whatever form they may adopt to teach or practice religion.

Justice Black added, however, that the New Jersey system of paying the bus fares of Roman Catholic school students did *not* violate these guidelines.

After its decision in the *Everson* case, the Supreme Court began to declare unconstitutional many of the ways that state laws regarded religion. One of the most important ways that states aided religion was by requiring prayers and religious exercises in public schools. During most of our nation's history, most teachers and parents believed that school prayer was important for teaching religious and ethical values to young children.

In the latter half of this century the United States has become more varied in its religious beliefs. Many people began to question school prayers. Some critics of school prayer came from minority religious groups. Many of these people opposed school prayer, since it usually reflected the beliefs of Protestants, who were members of the majority religion. Others also objected to school prayer since it violated their right not to believe in any religion.

The Supreme Court and School Prayer

The Supreme Court began to accept the views of those opposed to school prayer in the case of *Engel* v. *Vitale* (1962). Since 1951 the state of New York had required all public school students to recite the following prayer:

> Almighty God, we acknowledge our dependence upon Thee, and we beg Thy blessings upon us, our parents, our teachers and our Country.

Several students and parents in New Hyde Park, New York, objected to this prayer. They claimed that it violated the rights of nonbelievers and did not reflect the religious views of some believers.

The local school board refused to end the prayers. It did allow students to leave the room during the prayer if they wished. But this did not satisfy the prayer's opponents. They said that students who left the room during the prayer would be unfairly marked as "different" from the other students.

The case soon came before the Supreme Court. The Court agreed with the parents. In the words of Justice Hugo Black:

> It is neither sacrilegious [offensive] nor antireligious [against religions] to say that each separate government in this country should stay out of the business of writing or sanctioning [approving] official prayers and leave that purely religious function to the people themselves and to those the people look to for religious guidance.

The Court did not ban prayer in the schools. Students could still pray on their own. However, the Court did forbid any state-approved or teacher-led prayers. Following the *Engel* v. *Vitale* (1962) decision, the Court forbade other forms of state-approved religious activities in the schools. These included the reading of Bible verses and the saying of the Lord's Prayer.

These decisions let loose many criticisms of the Supreme Court. After the decision in the *Engel* case (1962), Congressman L. Mendel Rivers cried out, "The Court has now officially stated its disbelief in God Almighty." It is ironic that comments like this were leveled against a decision written by Justice Black, a very religious man and Sunday school teacher.

Those who opposed the Court's ruling attempted to undo it in various ways. One method was by calling for a constitutional amendment allowing school prayers. Since 1962, more than 300 amendments have been put forth to allow school prayer. None has received enough votes to pass Congress, however.

Some schools that wished to continue prayers made the practice voluntary. Other schools allowed a moment of silence. Students could use this moment for prayer or reflection. Many school districts simply ignored the Supreme Court and continued classroom prayers. By some estimates, teachers in more than half of the nation's school districts still lead their students in prayer.

The continuation of school prayer led to another important case in 1981. That September, five-year-old Chioke Jaffree came home from his kindergarten class in Mobile, Alabama. Chioke told his parents that he was upset. His teacher had led the class in singing grace before their lunch. Two of the Jaffrees' other children also said that their teachers had led them in prayer.

Chioke's father and mother, Ishmael and Mozelle Jaffree, had different religious beliefs. Ishmael was an agnostic, which means he was unsure of God's existence. Mozelle was of the Baha'i faith, a Middle Eastern religion based on Islam and Christianity. They had raised their children to choose their own religious beliefs, if any. Both parents agreed that their children's schools should not have classroom prayer.

Ishmael Jaffree told his children's teachers and their principals that he objected to the prayers. He pointed out that the Supreme Court had ruled school prayer unconstitutional. The schools still refused to stop the prayers. Ishmael then went to court to have the prayers stopped.

Ishmael Jaffree's lawsuit created a political storm in Alabama. Governor Forrest ("Fob") James went on television to criticize Ishmael Jaffree for trying to take prayer out of the schools. He then asked the state legislature to pass a law making voluntary prayer legal in Alabama's schools. The state legislature passed the law quickly.

The case went before a federal district court. The federal judge was W. Brevard Hand. Hand was very conservative. He allowed testimony from people who wanted to keep school prayer. He also allowed testimony from those who wanted to purge Alabama's textbooks of any ideas that they thought were antireligious.

Ishmael Jaffree's case was very simple. His lawyer argued that the Supreme Court had ruled more than twenty years earlier that school prayers were an unconstitutional establishment of religion. The Jaffrees claimed that Judge Hand was required to follow the precedent set by the Supreme Court and stop the prayers.

When Jaffree spoke in court he said, "I think children on their own should be free to pray before meals, at any time they want to." Jaffree's objection was to prayer led by teachers, since children are so easily impressed by adults. He said:

> They would accept a belief in the tooth fairy, just because it is told to them by adults. . . . I want my children not to accept everything that is told to them and be free to examine, to explore, to ponder, to think about, to be exposed to different philosophies.

Judge Hand ruled against Jaffree. He claimed that the First Amendment did not apply to the states. Judge Hand's reading of the Constitution contradicted fifty years of Supreme Court rulings. In his view, the Supreme Court could not stop Alabama from having

Ishmael Jaffree outside the federal district court in Mobile, Alabama, in 1982. Jaffree had gone to court to stop the schools from conducting prayers. The judge ruled that the First Amendment did not apply to the states, but the Supreme Court later ruled in Jaffree's favor.

prayer in its schools. Judge Hand also delivered a threat. If a higher court reversed his decision, he would start a campaign against the textbooks being used in Alabama's schools. He promised to ban any books that, in his view, promoted "anti-religious values."

Ishmael Jaffree then appealed his case to the federal appeals court. The higher federal courts do not approve of challenges like Judge Hand's that question their authority. The appeals court overturned the federal district court's decision, Judge Hand's decision. It told him that federal judges "are bound to adhere [stick] to the controlling decisions of the Supreme Court."

The state of Alabama then appealed the case to the U.S. Supreme Court. Alabama knew that the Supreme Court was unlikely to allow any teacher-led prayer. It then asked the Supreme Court to approve a state law allowing a one-minute silent prayer in the classroom. Alabama's lawyer argued that silent prayer did not force a student to violate his or her religious beliefs. He said, "During that minute he is in no way embarrassed, he is in no way coerced [forced] to do anything."

The Supreme Court voted to reverse Judge Hand's ruling and strike down Alabama's school prayer law. Most of the justices objected to Judge Hand's "remarkable conclusion that the Federal Constitution imposes no obstacle to Alabama's establishment of a state religion." Three justices agreed with Judge Hand that the First Amendment does not restrict the states from allowing silent prayer.

Liberals praised the Supreme Court's decision. But many conservatives criticized it as a blow against religion and moral values. The controversy did little to solve the question of prayer in schools. Many schools simply continued to ignore the Supreme Court. According to Ishmael Jaffree, "The teachers in my children's schools stopped saying the prayers, although I found out they were still praying in other schools."

Evolution and the Schools

Another important question involving the First Amendment's forbidding government support of religion also involves schools. For many years people have debated whether public schools can teach subjects that promote certain religious values. Most of the debate has focused on the teaching of evolution in public schools.

The idea of evolution has been controversial since 1859. In that year Charles Darwin first introduced the theory in his book *On the Origin of Species by Means of Natural Selection.* Darwin's theory proposes that plants and animals change or evolve over many millions of years as they adapt to their surroundings. His theory maintains that both apes and humans have evolved from a common ancestor.

Evolutionists disagree with those who make a literal interpretation of the Bible. Literal readers of the Bible are sometimes called fundamentalists. They believe that every word in the Bible is absolutely true, because it was inspired by God. They argue that Darwin must be wrong, since the Bible's Book of Genesis says all humans came from Adam and Eve, who were created by God. According to this, people could not have a common ancestor with apes. They also claim that, according to the Bible, Earth is much younger than the millions of years needed for evolution. These contradictions with the Bible have led many fundamentalists to argue that evolution is a sin against God.

Despite growing scientific evidence that supported evolution, many states early in this century passed laws that forbade its teaching in public schools. One such state was Tennessee. In 1925 John T. Scopes, a biology teacher in the small town of Dayton, decided to test Tennessee's law. He went ahead and explained evolution to his class. Scopes was then arrested and charged with violating the law.

The Scopes trial became a national event. Christian fundamentalists saw it as a chance for victory for their ideas. Scientists and supporters of free speech believed that the fundamentalists were antiscience. They hoped the trial would expose what they believed was the folly of the fundamentalists' view of creation.

The reputations of the trial's lawyers also added to its importance. Prosecuting Scopes for the Dayton school board was William Jennings Bryan. Bryan had been the Democratic nominee for president three times. He had also served as secretary of state in President Woodrow Wilson's cabinet. According to Bryan, "All the ills from which America suffers can be traced back to the teaching of evolution."

Defending Scopes was Clarence Darrow. Darrow was perhaps the most famous lawyer in the United States. He had become famous by representing many underdogs, including striking workers and political radicals.

The trial that Bryan called "a battle royal" went on for two weeks during the steamy Tennessee summer. Hundreds of reporters from around the world covered the trial. A parade of ministers and religious thinkers testified for and against the teaching of evolution.

The trial's climax came when Darrow called Bryan to the stand to testify as an expert on the Bible. Darrow's expert questioning of Bryan pointed out the problems of taking every word of the Bible literally. Bryan was unable to explain where Cain's wife had come from, since the only other people according to the Bible were his brother Abel and their parents, Adam and Eve.

It is unclear whether this exchange helped John Scopes. The jury found him guilty after only nine minutes of discussion. The judge fined him $100. Scopes's conviction was then reversed by the Tennessee Supreme Court on a technicality. Bryan's testimony probably convinced a wider audience around the nation that many views of the religious fundamentalists were contradictory and without scientific evidence.

The *Scopes* trial, the famous 1925 "monkey trial," was held in Dayton, Tennessee. Clarence Darrow is seated on the desk. John T. Scopes is seated to his immediate right. (His arms are interlocked, and he is looking straight ahead.) The trial received worldwide attention.

By 1965 only Mississippi and Arkansas still banned the teaching of evolution in their public schools. That year a Little Rock science teacher, Susan Epperson, decided to challenge the Arkansas law. She wanted to use a biology textbook that claimed that humans and apes "may have had a common, generalized ancestor in the remote past." According to Epperson, "This seemed to be a widely accepted theory and I feel it is my responsibility to acquaint my students with it."

The Supreme Court agreed with Susan Epperson. The Court voted that the Arkansas law violated the First Amendment's ban on the establishment of religion. It said the law promoted one particular religion's view of creation.

Justice Abe Fortas wrote the opinion for the Court. As a young boy in Tennessee he had followed the Scopes trial on the radio. He wrote that the state could not "prevent its teachers from discussing the theory of evolution because it is contrary to the belief of some that the Book of Genesis must be the exclusive source of doctrine as to the origins of man."

Susan Epperson's case did not end the controversy. In 1981 Arkansas and Louisiana passed laws saying that the teaching of evolution be given equal time in the classroom with the teaching of biblical versions of creation, known as creationism. Various religious, scientific, and legal groups banded together to fight these laws. In court, the respected scientist Stephen Jay Gould said that creationism "has no scientific factual basis or legitimate education purpose."

Arkansas and Louisiana could not match the scientific experts. One witness for the states said that comets from outer space brought life to Earth. Other advocates of creationism said that no matter how much scientific evidence there was, nothing could change their beliefs.

The Arkansas law was struck down in the lower federal courts in 1982. The case against the Louisiana law made it to the Supreme Court in 1987. Two justices—Chief Justice William Rehnquist and Justice Antonin Scalia—voted to uphold the Louisiana law. They

Susan Epperson, when she was a Little Rock, Arkansas, biology teacher, challenged the state's ban on teaching evolution in public schools. The Supreme Court declared the Arkansas ban unconstitutional.

argued that creationism "is a body of scientific knowledge," not just a religious belief. This opinion ignored the statement made by seventy-two Nobel Prize-winning scientists that creationism had no scientific evidence to support it.

The other seven justices voted to strike down Louisiana's law. Justice William Brennan wrote that Louisiana's law was equal to state support of religion, since it was intended "to advance the religious viewpoint that a supernatural being created humankind."

It seems likely that cases involving the First Amendment's ban on the establishment of religion will continue. As long as people deeply hold religious beliefs, they will want their schools to reflect those values. But as long as our nation remains one with many different religions and beliefs, then many people will fight against following any one set of ideas. The struggles between these two groups will shape our interpretation of the First Amendment. And the debates will continue to make the U.S. Constitution a living document.

The Free Exercise of Religion

"Compulsion by law of the acceptance of any creed or the practice of any form of worship is strictly forbidden. The freedom to hold religious beliefs and opinions is absolute."

CHIEF JUSTICE EARL WARREN,
in *Braunfeld* v. *Brown* (1961)

The First Amendment to the U.S. Constitution guarantees the free exercise of religion. But what does "free exercise" of religion mean? One part of the free exercise of religion is a person's right to believe in any religion that he or she wishes or to believe in no religion at all. No government law can force someone to change his or her beliefs about religion. This is one of the few absolute rights in the First Amendment.

The free exercise of religion also means that people have the right to act as their religion requires them to. Most actions caused by religious beliefs are also protected by the First Amendment. The government can, however, limit the right to exercise religious beliefs in special cases. For example, some religious sects rely on drugs or human sacrifices for their rituals. Obviously there is a good reason for the government to forbid these types of religious activities. Also, someone cannot invent his or her own religion. The First Amendment protects only established and accepted religious beliefs.

The First Latter-Day Saints in Missouri. The Mormons were one of a number of religious groups that suffered from persecution because people did not respect their First Amendment right to the free exercise of religion.

105

Questions about the lawfulness of religions and religious activities are central to the history of the First Amendment's free exercise clause. Many religious minorities have been denied their rights because people did not believe they were "real" religions. At other times people have tried to stop religious activities because they were angered or offended by them.

In the nineteenth century, members of the Church of Jesus Christ of Latter-Day Saints, also called Mormons, were persecuted for their religious beliefs. The Mormon religion was founded by Joseph Smith in 1830 after he claimed to have been visited by an angel. Smith and the Mormons tried to settle in Missouri, but townspeople chased them out. Many non-Mormons disliked parts of Mormonism. They were especially upset over the Mormon practice of polygamy (marriage to more than one wife).

The group then moved to Nauvoo, Illinois. Again, the Mormons found hostility to their religion. In 1844 Smith and his brother Hyrum were thrown in jail. There, an angry mob shot and killed them. Under the new leadership of Brigham Young, the Mormons moved west. In 1847 they founded Salt Lake City in what eventually became the state of Utah. Here the Mormons could practice their religion in peace.

Still the Mormons could not escape attempts to limit their religious freedom. In the 1870s, because of the Mormons, the federal government passed laws against polygamy in the western territories. In 1878 and 1889 the Supreme Court rejected attempts to have the laws ruled unconstitutional.

The Mormons argued that polygamy was a part of their religion and therefore protected by the First Amendment. The Supreme Court ruled otherwise. It said that polygamy was immoral and that allowing it would undermine society. In 1890, the Mormons forbade the practice of polygamy.

During this century in the United States, the Jehovah's Witnesses seem to have suffered the most from religious intolerance. The Jehovah's Witnesses began in the late 1800s. By the 1930s they had grown into a large religion. The Witnesses consider all other religions to be corrupt. They also believe that their mission is to preach their message in public and door-to-door.

The Witnesses also refuse to salute or pledge allegiance to the flag. They consider this a violation of the biblical commandment against worshipping anyone or anything but God. Many people disagreed with these beliefs and persecuted the Witnesses for them.

The first important case involving the Witnesses began in 1938 when three Witnesses, Newton Cantwell and his sons Jesse and Russell, were preaching their beliefs in New Haven, Connecticut. The Cantwells approached a group of people and asked them if they would listen to a phonograph record. The people agreed, and the Cantwells put on the record.

The record contained a speech denouncing all organized religions. The speech was especially critical of the Roman Catholic Church. Since the Cantwells were in a neighborhood with many Roman Catholics, it is no surprise that their record greatly angered the listeners.

The listeners told the Cantwells to turn off the record and to get out of the neighborhood. The listeners then informed the police of what had happened. The police arrested the Cantwells and charged them with disturbing the peace and soliciting (selling or appealing for) religious contributions without a permit.

Newton Cantwell took his case to the Supreme Court in 1940. He argued that he was just following his religious beliefs. He also said that his actions did not offer a "clear and present danger" to the public. Because of this, he claimed, the New Haven police had no right to arrest him.

The Supreme Court agreed with Cantwell. For the first time it "incorporated" the First Amendment's free exercise clause into the Fourteenth Amendment. This meant that the states as well as the federal government could not restrict the people's right to free exercise of their religion.

The Court held that the actions of the Cantwells should not have led to their arrests. It said that the Cantwells' record did not present a "clear and present danger" to the public. Just because it made the

Jehovah's Witnesses demonstrate in Texas in the 1940s. They were awaiting a hearing on their plea that they had been arrested without charges being filed. This religious group has been the center of several important Supreme Court cases.

listeners angry was not enough reason for the Cantwells' arrest. The Court also ruled that Connecticut could not require the Cantwells to get a permit to ask for contributions. In the opinion of the Court, it was not the place of the government to pick which religions could get a permit and which ones could not.

The Supreme Court's decision in favor of the Cantwells did not end the controversy over the Jehovah's Witnesses. Just two weeks after handing down the decision in the *Cantwell* case (1940), the Court moved to restrict the rights of the Witnesses. It ruled that Jehovah's Witness children in public schools could be forced to salute the flag even though doing so violated their religious beliefs. (See Chapter 1.)

Expanding the Definition of Religion

In time the Supreme Court reversed its decision in the flag salute case and broadened the right of the people to the free exercise of their religion. One way it has done this is by expanding the definition of religion to include previously excluded religions and beliefs. In 1944 the Court ruled in *United States* v. *Ballard* that even if a religious group made wild and absurd claims, government agencies could not restrict its religious activities. The case involved the "I Am" movement. It was led by Guy Ballard. At one point the movement had more than 3 million followers.

Ballard claimed that Jesus Christ had visited him. He also said that he and his relatives could cure incurable diseases. The federal government charged Ballard with fraud (deception) for mailing letters that boasted of these miracles and asked for money. Ballard claimed that the government could not determine if his claims were real, just as it could not determine if Moses had parted the Red Sea or if Jesus had risen from the dead.

The Supreme Court agreed with Ballard. Justice William O. Douglas wrote that the people's right to the free exercise of their religion

embraces [includes] the right to maintain theories of life and of death and of the hereafter which are rank heresy [religious lies] to followers of the orthodox [accepted] faiths. Men may believe what they cannot prove. . . . The religious views espoused by respondents [Ballard and his followers] might seem incredible, if not preposterous, to most people. But if those doctrines are subject to trial before a jury charged with finding their truth or falsity, then the same can be done with the religious beliefs of any sect.

In more recent years the Court has also expanded the activities it considers to be an exercise of religion. The Court has allowed Jehovah's Witnesses to ring doorbells in search of those who will listen to their sermons. The Court has also struck down many local "blue laws." These are laws that regulate the hours of business activities. The most common "blue laws" banned stores and other businesses from opening on Sundays.

Many religious groups, such as Jews and Seventh-Day Adventists, opposed "blue laws." Unlike members of many other faiths, members of these groups hold their religious services on days other than Sunday. Laws that kept them from opening their businesses on Sunday meant that they would lose the profits of two days instead of just one.

The Supreme Court has held that towns and states cannot enforce "blue laws" that discriminate against religious groups. Justice Potter Stewart wrote in 1961 that these laws force members of certain religions to make "a cruel choice . . . between . . . [their] religious faith and . . . [their] economic survival." He said that these laws are valid only if exceptions are made for those who have valid religious reasons for working on Sundays.

Free Exercise of Religion and Opposition to War

Opposition to war for religious reasons has been one of the most controversial issues regarding the free exercise clause. Many religions hold pacifist, or antiwar, beliefs. Followers of these religions believe that war and violence are immoral. The members of these religious groups believe that fighting in the armed forces is a sin, even in the defense of one's country. People who refuse to fight on religious grounds are usually known as conscientious objectors, or COs.

Many pacifists have suffered for their views. During World War I, pacifists were thrown in prison or attacked by angry mobs. In World War II and the Korean War, Congress defined conscientious objectors as those whose belief in a Supreme Being kept them from going to war.

During the Vietnam War in the 1960s, many young men claimed to be conscientious objectors. Many did so even though their opposition to war did not come from a belief in God or a

An early American Quaker meeting. Many members of this religious group have opposed war for religious reasons.

Supreme Being. These men opposed war for personal moral reasons, not religious ones. One of these young men was Dan Seeger. Even though his case began before the Vietnam War, the issues it raised were similar to many others during that war.

In 1957 Dan Seeger wrote a letter to his local draft board telling it that he thought war was immoral and unethical. He therefore would refuse to serve in the military. The draft board then sent Seeger a form to apply for conscientious objector status. One question on the form asked if he believed in a Supreme Being. The question was followed by two boxes, one marked "yes" and the other marked "no." Seeger drew in and checked his own box. The box said, "Please see attached sheets."

Dan Seeger had attached seven single-spaced, typewritten pages to answer the question. His answer said a simple yes or no could not explain his views. Seeger argued that he did not deny the existence of a Supreme Being. But he could not say with honest certainty that he believed in one. He also wrote that his religious beliefs did not have to rely on a belief in God.

The draft board rejected Dan Seeger's request for CO status. It claimed that the draft excluded only those whose belief in a Supreme Being made them object to war. It then told Seeger that he had to report to the military.

Seeger took his case to court. He argued that the draft board was forcing him to violate his religious beliefs. He said that the government could not reject a religious philosophy just because it did not state a belief in a Supreme Being. Seeger claimed that he held his beliefs just as deeply and sincerely as those who believed in God.

Dan Seeger's case finally made its way to the Supreme Court in 1965. The Court agreed with Seeger. When the justices met to decide how to vote, Chief Justice Earl Warren said, "I don't know how to define 'Supreme Being' and judges perhaps ought not to do so." Conservative Justice John Marshall Harlan agreed. He said Congress could not "pick and choose between religious beliefs."

Justice Tom C. Clark wrote the Court's opinion in the case *United States* v. *Seeger* (1965). He said that the government could not draft conscientious objectors simply because their religious beliefs did not include a belief in God. He stated that the government could not draft men like Dan Seeger who held "a sincere and meaningful belief" similar to a belief in God. Drafting them, Justice Clark claimed, would violate their right to free exercise of religion.

Five years later the Court went further. It said that men who opposed war on purely ethical or moral grounds, not religious ones, must also be exempted from the draft. Justice Hugo Black wrote that the First Amendment protected such views. He said that men who held such ethical views "with the strength of more traditional religious convictions" could be exempted from the draft.

As the Vietnam War continued, more and more Americans began to oppose it. Many men felt that the war was unjust and therefore refused to fight. Some claimed that they would fight in other, just wars, but not in an unjust war like that in Vietnam.

The Supreme Court in 1971 rejected this argument. It ruled that those who wished to be conscientious objectors had to oppose all wars, not only the wars they viewed as unjust. The Court said that there was no way to distinguish people who sincerely believed a war was unjust from those who merely made that claim to avoid military service.

Religious and philosophical views are among our most intensely private beliefs. It is probably safe to say that no two people hold exactly the same views on these matters. And each person's view requires him or her to act or not to act in different ways. As long as our nation is home to such a wide variety of beliefs, we will continue to debate the meaning of the First Amendment's free exercise clause.

Freedom of the Press: Prior Restraint

"Were it left to me to decide whether we should have a government without newspapers or newspapers without a government, I should not hesitate for a moment to prefer the latter."

THOMAS JEFFERSON, 1787

The Framers of our Bill of Rights knew that the First Amendment's guarantee of the people's right to free expression would be of little use if the amendment did not also guarantee their right to a free press. The right to speak out on ideas and issues is important and powerful. But its impact is limited. The human voice can travel only so far, and it is heard for only a moment. But when ideas are printed in books and newspapers or broadcast over radio and television, they can reach millions. Their impact can last for many years.

A free press also serves another function for a democracy. Few people can stay in Washington and constantly check on what the government is doing. A free press helps to keep the public informed of the activities of government. Without this information, the public would not have the information necessary to control the government. Thomas Jefferson said that the people must be given

---

A printing press. One way that governments in many parts of the world attempt to censor the press is by prior restraint. Prior restraint is any system that gives public officials the power to deny freedom of speech or freedom of the press in advance of actual expression.

full information of their affairs thru the channel of the public papers, & to contrive [plan] that those papers should penetrate the whole mass of the people. . . . Were it left to me to decide whether we should have a government without newspapers or newspapers without a government, I should not hesitate for a moment to prefer the latter.

The First Amendment says that Congress shall make no law abridging or limiting freedom of the press. There are a number of ways governments may try to limit freedom of the press. Sometimes they try to ban certain writings by preventing their sale after they have been published. Other methods call for reviewing manuscripts and preventing publication of manuscripts they disapprove of. This form of censorship is also called prior restraint.

Jay Near's Newspaper and Freedom of the Press

The first important case concerning prior restraint to reach the U.S. Supreme Court began in Minneapolis, Minnesota, in 1927. Corruption was common in Minneapolis in the 1920s. Prohibition had made the sale of alcohol illegal in the United States. Gangsters smuggled crates of alcohol across the Canadian border into Minneapolis and then on to Chicago and St. Louis. These gangsters also ran a chain of speakeasies (illegal saloons), gambling dens, and other illegal activities in Minneapolis. To make sure that there was no interference with their activities, the gangsters paid off many local politicians. Minneapolis's mayor, chief of police, and district attorney were paid by the gangsters to ignore what was happening.

Into this picture stepped Howard Guilford and Jay Near. Ten years before, Guilford and Near had published the *Twin City Reporter*. The *Reporter* was a graphic newspaper full of gossip and tales of scandal involving well-known Minneapolis citizens. The newspaper also made regular attacks on minorities, especially Jews, African Americans, and Roman Catholics. Despite its gossip and racial and religious prejudices, the paper did help to expose corruption in the city government.

Near and Guilford eventually sold the *Reporter* and went their separate ways. In 1927 they decided to go back into the newspaper business. Their new paper was called the *Saturday Press*. Given Near and Guilford's past actions, the Minneapolis chief of police, Frank Brunskill, ordered his men to keep the paper off the streets. Chief Brunskill had no authority to do this.

Minneapolis gangsters also felt threatened by the paper. They tried to kill Guilford for denouncing them in his paper. Guilford was shot four times, but survived.

Despite Chief Brunskill's orders and the attempt on Guilford's life, Jay Near continued to publish the newspaper. In fact, his stories became even more outspoken. He accused Minneapolis mayor George Leach, county attorney Floyd Olson, and Chief Brunskill of accepting payoffs from local gangsters. Near also claimed that Jews operated the local crime gangs. At one point Near wrote:

> There have been too many men in this city and especially those in official life, who HAVE been taking orders and suggestions from JEW GANGSTERS, therefore we HAVE Jew Gangsters, practically running Minneapolis. . . .
>
> I simply state a fact when I say that ninety per cent of the crimes committed against society in this city are committed by Jew gangsters.

With statements such as this, Near finally provoked local officials into shutting down his newspaper. In November 1927, county attorney Floyd Olson (later the governor of Minnesota) asked Hennepin County judge Mathias Baldwin to forbid further publication of the *Saturday Press*. Olson cited a 1925 Minnesota law against "malicious, scandalous, and defamatory newspaper[s]." This law was known as the "gag law." It was intended to gag, or silence, any disagreeable newspapers.

Olson claimed that the *Saturday Press* had defamed, that is, harmed the reputation of, Mayor Leach, Chief Brunskill, himself, and the entire Jewish community of Minneapolis. Judge Baldwin agreed and ordered Near to stop publication. Near went along with Judge Baldwin's order. But he believed that the action was unconstitutional.

Near then appealed his case to the Minnesota Supreme Court. He claimed that the "gag law" violated the free press guarantees of the Minnesota constitution and the First Amendment of the U.S. Constitution. Near also tried to show that many of his accusations about official corruption were true.

In May the Minnesota Supreme Court ruled against Near. The chief justice of the Minnesota Supreme Court, Samuel Bailey Wilson, wrote:

> Liberty of the press does not mean that an evil-minded person may publish just anything any more than the constitutional right of free assembly authorizes and legalizes unlawful assemblies and riots.

Bailey recognized that some of what Near had published was true, but he said, "There is no constitutional right to publish a fact merely because it is true."

The Right to Publish Is Debated

Jay Near's case attracted the attention of two unlikely and very different figures. One of them was Roger Baldwin, founder of the American Civil Liberties Union (ACLU). He set up the ACLU to help protect the people's First Amendment rights.

Baldwin strongly disagreed with most of what Jay Near published. Yet he believed that a free press gave Near the right to publish what he wanted without government censorship. He believed that if the government could stop Jay Near, then it could also censor more respectable newspapers. Baldwin spent the ACLU's money to appeal Near's case to the U.S. Supreme Court.

Near's case also caught the attention of Colonel Robert R. McCormick, the publisher of the *Chicago Tribune*. Colonel McCormick was very conservative. The front page of each *Tribune*

Roger Baldwin in 1970. He founded the American Civil Liberties Union in 1920 and was its controversial director from 1920 to 1950.

carried the motto "Our country, right or wrong." McCormick used his newspaper to attack any person or group he believed to be un-American or Communist.

McCormick was also a strong believer in the First Amendment and the people's right to a free press. Like Near he had fought local officials who disliked his attacks. While most of the nation's major newspapers ignored the *Near* case or applauded the banning of the *Saturday Press,* McCormick decided to help Near in his appeal. He gave Near expert legal help and the funds needed to pay for his case. McCormick also had the *Tribune* run many articles and editorials claiming Near's innocence and supporting the people's right to a free press.

Jay Near's case finally reached the Supreme Court on January 30, 1931. Near's attorney, Weymouth Kirkland, argued that the Minnesota law banning the *Saturday Press* was unconstitutional. He said that the Fourteenth Amendment kept the states from limiting freedom of the press, just as the First Amendment prevented the federal government from doing the same. Kirkland went on to claim that the state of Minnesota could not use prior restraint.

Presenting the case for Minnesota was Deputy Attorney General James Markham. He said that the Minnesota law was not unconstitutional. Markham held that the law did not violate the rights of legitimate newspapers. Markham claimed that it merely prevented the publication of scandalous newspapers like Near's.

The Supreme Court decided in Jay Near's favor by the close vote of 5 to 4. Chief Justice Charles Evans Hughes knew the importance of this case and decided to write the opinion himself. Reading the opinion before the Court, Hughes said, "It is no longer open to doubt that the liberty of the press and of speech is within the liberty safeguarded by the due process clause of the Fourteenth Amendment from invasion by state action." From now on neither the states nor the federal government could violate the people's right to free speech and press.

Hughes then stated that while some might abuse the privilege of a free press, this risk was outweighed by the need of the free press to expose corruption and misdeeds in government. He said, "The fact that liberty of the press may be abused by miscreant purveyors [evil providers] of scandal does not make any the less necessary the immunity of the press from previous restraint in dealing with official misconduct." If what Near had printed was untrue then he could be punished for it after publication, not before.

The case of *Near* v. *Minnesota* (1931) was a triumph for the defenders of free speech. The Supreme Court had protected freedom of the press from state violations. It had also held that government could not censor or exercise prior restraint over the press.

Freedom of the Press versus National Security: The Pentagon Papers

As with most other freedoms, the Supreme Court did not consider the freedom from censorship to be absolute. In *Near* v. *Minnesota* (1931), Chief Justice Charles Evans Hughes had stated that the government in time of war or other emergency could censor a newspaper that published information damaging to the national security. It would take another forty years before the Supreme Court would attempt to define the line where freedom of the press ended and national security began.

The United States in 1971 was bitterly divided. The war in Vietnam had dragged on into its seventh year. It was about to become our longest war. At first most Americans supported the war. But as more and more Americans died and victory seemed less and less likely, many came to believe that the war was both unwinnable and unjust.

One of these people was Daniel Ellsberg. He had worked for the government and had spent much time in Vietnam. There, he had advised the government on how to win the war. As time went by, he became less sure of his views. Ellsberg came to believe that the war was wrong. He believed that the government had lied to the American people.

Ellsberg knew of a secret government study of the history of the war. This study, which became known as the Pentagon Papers, showed that the government had misinformed the American people about its goals in the war and its chances of victory. Ellsberg stole the report and gave copies of it to the *New York Times,* the *Washington Post,* and other newspapers.

On June 13, 1971, the *New York Times* began printing the first part of a planned five-part series based on the Pentagon Papers. The federal government, under orders from President Richard Nixon, went to court to prevent the newspapers from publishing the study. This was the first time in U.S. history that the federal government had asked for such prior restraint. The Nixon administration claimed that publication of this secret information would result in "the death of soldiers, the destruction of alliances, the greatly increased difficulty of negotiation with our enemies, the inability of our diplomats to negotiate," and the lengthening of the war. Federal district courts refused to allow the government to prevent further publication of the study. But the federal government then appealed to the next level of federal courts—the courts of appeal. One of the courts of appeals ordered the *New York Times* to stop publishing the Pentagon Papers articles. It said that the government needed time to prepare its case against the newspaper.

The *New York Times* and other newspapers that had received copies of the Pentagon Papers claimed that the study presented no threat to national security. They argued that the history studied in the papers ended in 1968 and contained no information that could threaten the war effort in 1971. They also said that the public had a right to know the facts of the war and whether the government had lied.

The *New York Times* had been ordered to temporarily stop printing the Pentagon Papers articles. Within days, the newspaper appealed to the Supreme Court. The Supreme Court acted quickly. It knew that the executive branch of the government could tie up the case in court for months or years. This would have the practical effect of censoring the newspapers, or keeping them from publishing anything that did not have the approval of the government.

Seventeen days after the Pentagon Papers first appeared in print, the Supreme Court decided that the government could not stop their publication.

Three justices ruled that the government could stop publication of the study. Justice Harry Blackmun wrote that the Court had acted too quickly in deciding the case. He also argued that freedom of the press was no more important than the right of the president to conduct foreign policy and to protect the nation's security.

Six justices ruled that publication of the Pentagon Papers could continue, but for different reasons. Justices Hugo Black and William O. Douglas ruled that the government could not censor the press under any circumstances. Black wrote:

> The press was protected by the First Amendment so that it could bare the secrets of government and inform the people. Only a free and unrestrained [unrestricted] press can effectively expose deception in government. . . .
>
> Paramount [highest] among the responsibilities of a free press is the duty to prevent any part of the Government from deceiving the people and sending them off to distant lands to die of foreign fevers and foreign shot and shell. In my view, far from deserving condemnation for their courageous reporting, *The New York Times, The Washington Post,* and other newspapers should be commended [praised] for serving the purpose that the Founding Fathers saw so clearly. In revealing the workings of Government that led to the Vietnam war, the newspapers nobly did precisely that which the Founders hoped and trusted they would do. . . .
>
> The guarding of military and diplomatic secrets at the expense of informed representative government provides no real security for our Republic.

Four other justices, William Brennan, Potter Stewart, Byron White, and Thurgood Marshall, all agreed that government could not stop publication of the Pentagon Papers. Justice Stewart wrote that nothing in them would "surely result in direct, immediate, and irreparable [permanent] damage to our Nation and its people."

Daniel and Patricia Ellsberg. Daniel Ellsberg had released the government study known as the Pentagon Papers to the press in 1971. In that year, the Supreme Court ruled that the government could not prevent newspapers from publishing the Pentagon Papers. In 1973, the case against Daniel Ellsberg was dismissed.

Unlike Black and Douglas, these justices did not believe that the people's right to a free press was absolute. For example, Justice Brennan wrote that the government could prevent the publication of secret information such as "the sailing dates of transports or the number and location of troops."

Freedom of the Press and the Right to a Fair Trial

Just as the Supreme Court has attempted to balance the rights of a free press with the needs of national security, they have also tried to balance freedom of the press with other rights provided in the Bill of Rights. One of these rights is the Sixth Amendment's guarantee of the right to a fair trial. An important case involving the conflict between these two rights came in 1976 in the case of *Nebraska Press Association* v. *Stuart*.

The case began in 1975 when Erwin Charles Simants was arrested and charged with murdering six members of a family in Sutherland, Nebraska. The judge in the trial, Hugh Stuart, worried that the publicity surrounding such a terrible crime might prevent Simants from getting a fair trial. To stop this publicity, Judge Stuart placed a "gag order" keeping the press from releasing certain information in the case. The Nebraska Press Association appealed this ruling. The association said that it was an unconstitutional example of prior restraint.

In 1976 all nine members of the Supreme Court agreed. Chief Justice Burger wrote the opinion of the Court. They decided that Judge Stuart's order violated the rights of a free press. Burger did, however, indicate that there might be situations where the Court would allow a judge to place a "gag order" to ensure a fair trial.

In 1990 the Supreme Court allowed a judge's "gag order" in the trial of General Manuel Noriega, former leader of Panama. The case began in 1989, following the invasion of Panama by the U.S. military. Noriega was captured and brought to the United States to stand trial for drug smuggling. While Noriega was in jail, the government made tapes of him talking with his lawyers. Cable

News Network (CNN) obtained copies of these tapes and broadcast parts of them in 1990.

General Noriega's lawyers claimed that broadcasting these tapes might prevent him from getting a fair trial. They said the tapes revealed private discussions related to his legal defense. They asked federal district court judge William H. Hoeveler to order CNN to stop broadcasting the tapes until it could be determined if there was anything in them that might prevent a fair trial. CNN argued that the order to stop broadcasting the tapes was an unconstitutional example of prior restraint. The network cited the Supreme Court's decision in the *Stuart* case.

On November 8, Judge Hoeveler ordered CNN to stop broadcasting the tapes and to hand them over for review. A federal appeals court let Judge Hoeveler's decision stand. CNN then appealed the case to the Supreme Court.

A few days later, seven justices voted to uphold the ban on broadcasting the tapes until Judge Hoeveler could determine if the tapes contained information that might prevent General Noriega from receiving a fair trial. Justices Thurgood Marshall and Sandra Day O'Connor strongly disagreed with the rest of the Court. They claimed that the Court's decision went against its previous ruling in the *Stuart* case. The lower federal court, within a few days, allowed CNN to play the tapes. But the Supreme Court's decision in this case is almost certain to lead to further controversy and debate over how to balance freedom of the press with the right to a fair trial.

Freedom of the Press and Student Newspapers

Important issues about freedom of the press do not always involve powerful institutions and burning national issues, as in the *Pentagon Papers* case or the Noriega trial. Often, freedom of the press has involved ordinary students across the United States. Some of the most important decisions about a free press have involved student newspapers and the right of schools to censor them, or keep them from publishing anything that did not have the approval of the schools.

One important case of freedom of the press for student newspapers involved two high school students in Fairfax County, Virginia. In 1976 Lauren Boyd and Gina Gambino were editors of their high school's newspaper. Lauren and Gina decided to write an article for their newspaper that discussed how many sexually active students did not use birth control.

When the school principal decided to censor the article, Lauren and Gina decided to fight back. They took their case to court. They argued that censorship of the student newspaper was a clear violation of their First Amendment rights.

The school board said the article violated its policy against teaching sex education. It also claimed that school officials should be able to control the content of student newspapers. School officials feared the newspaper might become a scandal sheet, full of false information and shocking details. They asked, "Should not the school administration, which is expert in educating and understanding children, be able to exercise reasonable editorial control of the official student newspaper?"

The courts agreed with Lauren and Gina. Federal Judge Albert Bryan, Jr., wrote, "The state cannot constitutionally restrict anyone's First Amendment rights, including those of students, because of mere apprehension [fear] of what they might do with them." Judge Bryan's decision was later upheld by the federal court of appeals. The school board then decided not to take the case to the U.S. Supreme Court.

Despite the success of Lauren and Gina, censorship of student newspapers continues. A 1974 study stated:

Censorship and the systematic lack of freedom to engage in open, responsible journalism characterize high school [newspapers]. Unconstitutional and arbitrary restraints [by school officials] are so deeply imbedded [planted] in high school journalism as to overshadow its achievement.

By taking their case to court, Lauren and Gina were exceptions. Very few cases involving censorship of student newspapers ever go to court. There are several reasons for this. Many students are not aware of their First Amendment rights. Others think that these rights apply only to adults and not to students. In still other cases, students decide not to protest censorship out of fear of getting into trouble with school officials or hurting their chances of getting into college.

The Supreme Court in 1988 gave school officials broader control over student newspapers. The case began in a suburb near St. Louis, Missouri. The principal of Hazelwood High School censored two articles written for the student newspaper. The articles discussed teenage pregnancy and the impact of divorce on children at the school. Students in a journalism class wrote and edited the newspaper as part of the high school's curriculum. The principal believed that one article's discussion of sexual activity and birth control might not be suitable for the younger students. He also thought that the unnamed pregnant students might be identified from the article. The principal also thought a father described in the divorce article did not have an opportunity to present his side of the divorce.

Justice Byron White wrote the majority opinion of the Supreme Court for *Hazelwood School District* v. *Kuhlmeier* (1988). He said that schools had the right to censor any *school-sponsored activities,* including student newspapers. Principals and school boards could censor anything that they believed did not reflect the school's "basic educational mission." All they needed to show was that the activity was "reasonably related" to educational concerns.

Justices Brennan, Marshall, and Blackmun disagreed with the rest of the Court. Justice Brennan wrote that the Court's decision robbed students of their First Amendment rights. He went on to say, "Instead of teaching children to respect the diversity [variety] of ideas that is fundamental to the American system, the Court today 'teaches youth to discount important principles of our government as mere platitudes [meaningless words].'"

The examples of censorship of student newspapers show that debate over the people's right to a free press is very much alive. These examples also show that protection of our First Amendment rights often come from ordinary people like Lauren Boyd and Gina Gambino, who have fought for their rights.

Freedom of the Press: Libel

"The First Amendment requires that we protect some falsehoods in order to protect speech that matters."

JUSTICE LEWIS F. POWELL, JR.,
in *Gertz* v. *Robert Welch, Inc.* (1974)

The cases discussed in Chapter 9 show that the U.S. Supreme Court has been unwilling to let the government use censorship or prior restraint over the press. But the people's right to a free press is not absolute. The First Amendment does not protect publishers of libel. Libel is the publication of false information that is damaging to a person's job or good name. An example of libel would be if a school's newspaper falsely accused a student of cheating on a test.

The government cannot forbid the publication of what it thinks is libel. However, victims of libel can ask courts to force their accusers to pay for any damages they suffered. Though this system seems fair and just, it also can be abused in ways that limit the people's right to a free press. One example of this began in 1960.

New York Times v. *Sullivan* (1964)

On March 20, 1960, the *New York Times* printed a full-page ad paid for by many important people, including African-American minis-

---

Associate Justice William Brennan served on the Supreme Court from 1956 to 1990. He wrote the majority opinion in a 1964 case that limited state power in cases where public officials sued citizens who criticized those officials' public duties. He wrote that "debate on public issues should be . . . wide open, and . . . might include vehement, caustic, and sometimes unpleasantly sharp attacks on government and public officials."

ters from the South. The ad was titled "Heed Their Rising Voices." Its aim was to tell readers of the struggle African Americans in the South faced as they tried to win their civil rights. One section of the ad read:

> In Montgomery, Alabama, after students sang, "My Country, 'Tis of Thee" on the State Capitol steps, their leaders were expelled from school, and truckloads of police armed with shotguns and tear-gas ringed the Alabama State College Campus. When the entire student body protested to state authorities by refusing to re-register, their dining hall was padlocked in an attempt to starve them into submission . . . .

> Again and again the Southern violators have answered [civil rights leader] Dr. [Martin Luther] King's peaceful protests with intimidation and violence. They have bombed his home almost killing his wife and child. They have assaulted his person. They have arrested him seven times—for "speeding," "loitering," and similar "offenses." And now they have charged him with "perjury"—a *felony* under which they could imprison him for *ten years*.

When L. B. Sullivan, head of the Montgomery police, read this he decided to sue the *New York Times* for libel. According to Sullivan, the ad obviously referred to him, though his name was not mentioned. He claimed it falsely tied him to those who had bombed Dr. King's home and beaten him. He also pointed out that the ad contained the following mistakes:

- The students sang "The Star-Spangled Banner," not "My Country, 'Tis of Thee."
- Students were expelled from school for refusing to leave a segregated lunch counter, not for protesting at the state capitol.
- The Montgomery police were stationed near the campus, not around it.
- The cafeteria was not locked.
- Police arrested Dr. King four times, not seven.

Sullivan took his case to court in Alabama and won. An all-white jury awarded him $500,000. The *Times* decided to appeal the case to the U.S. Supreme Court. The Court agreed with the *Times* and said that the ad did not libel Sullivan.

Justice William Brennan wrote the Court's unanimous (9 to 0) decision in *New York Times Co.* v. *Sullivan* (1964). He said that the First Amendment meant "debate on public issues should be uninhibited, robust, and wide open . . . ." Because of this, "Erroneous [mistaken] statement is inevitable in free debate, and must be protected if the freedoms of expression are to have the 'breathing space' that they 'need . . . to survive.'"

Montgomery, Alabama, police commissioner L. B. Sullivan (second from the left) celebrates his $500,000 libel suit victory over the *New York Times*. However, the U.S. Supreme Court later unanimously reversed the Alabama Supreme Court's decision.

Without this "breathing space," the right to criticize public officials would be restricted. Brennan wrote that publishers who faced paying huge sums of money if they printed even the smallest of errors might use "self-censorship" and refuse to print any controversial materials. According to Brennan, such a system "dampens the vigor and limits the variety of public debate. It is inconsistent with the First and Fourteenth Amendments."

Brennan added that public officials could still sue for libel. But now they had to show that their accusers were guilty of "actual malice." This meant that the accusers knew that what they were saying was false or they didn't care if what they were saying was false or not. Brennan stated that there was no evidence that the sponsors of the ad or the *New York Times* had acted with malice toward L. B. Sullivan. Therefore the Court threw out the suit.

After this the Supreme Court began to expand its ruling to cover not just public officials, but also private citizens involved in important public matters and issues. But the Court's decision in *New York Times Co.* v. *Sullivan* (1964) left open the question of who was a public figure and who was a private citizen. Could the news media spread false information about ordinary citizens? If these citizens sued for libel, would they have to prove malice?

The Case of Elmer Gertz

The Supreme Court tried to answer these questions in 1974. The case began in 1969 when Elmer Gertz, a Chicago lawyer, received a pamphlet printed by the John Birch Society. This ultraconservative organization began in the McCarthy era. Its members are devoted to fighting communism in America. Over the years they have accused many Americans of Communist connections, including Presidents Franklin Roosevelt and Dwight D. Eisenhower.

A shocked Gertz saw his picture in the pamphlet. Also in the pamphlet were statements that he was a Communist with a criminal record who was trying to destroy the police across the United States. The author of the article, Alan Stang, charged that Gertz was a member of "the Communist National Lawyers Guild." He added that Gertz had tried to frame Chicago police officer Richard Nuccio. The policeman had been convicted of the murder of Ronald Nelson.

It was true that Gertz had been a member of the Lawyers Guild. But this group was not Communist. Many lawyers had joined it, including three members of the Supreme Court. In addition, Gertz had quit the Lawyers Guild over fifteen years earlier. Also, Gertz had no criminal record. Finally, Gertz's only association with the *Nuccio* case was that he had helped the Nelson family to receive damages from Nuccio after his conviction. He had nothing to do with Nuccio's murder conviction. Because of this, Gertz decided to sue Stang and the John Birch Society for libel.

Elmer Gertz's case shows how two important rights can often conflict. Private citizens like Elmer Gertz have the right to keep their names from being tarred by false accusations like those of the John Birch Society. But the First Amendment allows the press, even when it is run by a fringe group like the John Birch Society, to spread its opinions on important topics. If publishers had to prove every point they made, then they might be slow to speak out on controversial issues.

The decision in *Gertz* v. *Robert Welch, Inc.* (1974) depended upon whether or not Gertz was a public figure. If Gertz were a public figure, then he would have to follow the rule set down in *New York Times Co.* v. *Sullivan* (1964). This meant he would have to prove the difficult charge that Stang and the John Birch Society acted with malice. If the courts ruled Gertz was not a public figure, then he would have to prove only that the charges were false.

Both the federal district court and the federal court of appeals ruled that Gertz was a public figure. These courts said that Gertz had become a public figure by representing Ronald Nelson's family in a case that was an important public controversy. As a result, Gertz had to show that the John Birch Society was guilty of malice. The courts said that he had not done this. There was no evidence that the John Birch Society knew the article was untrue.

Elmer Gertz, whose case was decided by the Supreme Court in 1974. Private citizens such as Gertz needed to prove only that a publisher failed to exercise normal care in checking out facts before printing damaging falsehoods. If such private citizens could prove that, they might receive payment for actual injuries to their reputation.

Gertz then appealed his case to the U.S. Supreme Court. The Court issued its opinion in June 1974. Justice Lewis Powell defined a public figure as someone who achieves such "fame and notoriety [bad reputation] that he becomes a public figure." A public figure also might be someone who becomes involved in a "public controversy." Powell added that the First Amendment protected the people's right to make false statements about public figures. He said, "The First Amendment requires that we protect some false-hoods in order to protect speech that matters."

Powell then ruled that Gertz was a private citizen, not a public figure. According to Powell, "He [Gertz] plainly did not thrust himself into the vortex [center] of this public issue, nor did he engage the public's attention in an attempt to influence its outcome." The Court then ruled that Gertz deserved a new trial. Finally, in 1981, seven years after the Supreme Court's decision and twelve years after the incident began, a jury agreed that the John Birch Society had libeled Gertz. The jury then ordered the society to pay Gertz $400,000 in damages. Elmer Gertz had finally cleared his name.

The Supreme Court's ruling in *New York Times Co.* v. *Sullivan* (1964) also raised another important question. To determine if they acted with malice, can courts order journalists to reveal their "state of mind"? In other words, do journalists have to tell what they were thinking about when they put together a story?

The Supreme Court answered yes to this question in 1979. The case began when the CBS News program "60 Minutes" broadcast a report critical of U.S. Army Colonel Anthony Herbert. Colonel Herbert then decided to sue CBS and CBS producer Barry Lando for libel.

Herbert's lawyer charged that "the broadcast was a deliberately selective presentation directed at creating but a single impression—that Herbert was a liar, an opportunist, and a brutal person." Because of the story, Herbert's lawyer claimed Herbert's "reputation and good name were destroyed and he suffered severe financial losses."

Herbert asked the court to force Lando to answer questions about his "state of mind" regarding the story and Colonel Herbert. The questions tried to find out why Lando had not included material favorable to Colonel Herbert. Herbert said this line of questioning was needed to find out if Lando was guilty of malice. Lando, who answered all other questions, refused to answer any questions about his "state of mind."

The U.S. Supreme Court decided the case in 1979. Three justices voted to support CBS producer Barry Lando. They said that what he did or did not think about the case did not matter. What *did* matter was whether or not the information in the story was false and if Lando had known this or had recklessly ignored it.

Six other justices disagreed. They voted to allow "state of mind" questions. Justice Byron White wrote the Court's opinion. He said that it was only fair that a person who claimed to have been libeled should be able to probe the thoughts of a journalist to find out if he had recklessly ignored the truth.

Journalists around the country protested the Court's decision against CBS. They claimed that the decision would have a "chilling effect" on their work. They might not want to cover controversial stories for fear of being sued for libel.

In 1990 the Supreme Court again limited the First Amendment's protection of the people's right to make uninhibited statements. The case involved a sports reporter for a small newspaper in Ohio. The reporter accused a high school coach of lying to a grand jury investigating a fight at a sporting event. The coach then sued the newspaper for libel.

The newspaper stated that the charges against the coach appeared in an editorial column, not a news story. An editorial column is used to state opinions, not to report the facts of the news. Therefore, the newspaper argued, the charges were merely offered as opinion, not as hard facts. In the view of the newspaper, stating an opinion cannot be considered libel.

The Supreme Court disagreed. By a vote of 7 to 2, the Court held that stating an opinion could be viewed as libel. The Court did say that the First Amendment protected expressions of opinion that did not contain "a provably false factual connotation [meaning]."

The debate over the limits to the protection of libel in the First Amendment continues. There is a delicate balance between a person's right to be free from false accusations and the people's need for a free press. The balance between the two has changed as different people acting at different times have argued the question. As people and times change, the balance will also change. As it does, we will continue to debate the exact meaning and extent of the guarantee of the people's rights in the First Amendment.

Freedom of Expression: Obscenity

"There are as many different definitions of obscenity as there are men; and they are as unique to the individual as his dreams."

JUSTICE WILLIAM O. DOUGLAS, 1971

The previous chapters showed that the people's right to free expression is not absolute. A person cannot say something that causes a "clear and present danger" to the public. Publishers cannot print news stories that might damage national security in time of war. Nor can a person publish information that libels, or falsely accuses, a private citizen.

In the view of the U.S. Supreme Court, freedom of the press does not protect the publishers of obscene materials either. Something is obscene if it is deeply offensive, immoral, disgusting, or shocking. An example might be a vivid description of a violent act. Others regard sexually descriptive materials to be obscene.

There has never been a precise legal definition of obscenity. Books or films that some regard as repulsive are often seen by others as mildly annoying. Others may even view the same books or films as works of art. In 1971 Justice William O. Douglas wrote, "There are as many different definitions of obscenity as there are men; and they are as unique to the individual as his dreams."

Justice Potter Stewart also saw how personal standards are involved in defining obscenity. In a 1964 case dealing with a potentially obscene film he wrote:

Protesters demand an end to attempts to censor artworks as obscene.

I shall not today attempt further to define the kinds of material I understand to be embraced within that ... description [of obscenity]; and perhaps I never could succeed in intelligibly [clearly] doing so. But I know it when I see it, and the motion picture involved in this case is not that.

In other words, Justice Stewart was saying, "I can't define obscenity, but I know it when I see it."

The failure to define obscenity has troubled the Supreme Court over the years. The Court first attempted this in 1957. The case *Roth* v. *United States* involved Samuel Roth. He was arrested and convicted of breaking a federal law against sending obscene materials through the mail.

Roth appealed his conviction to the Supreme Court. There, his lawyers argued that the First Amendment protected all forms of expression, even those that could be considered obscene. The Supreme Court disagreed. It stated that the First Amendment protected many things, but not obscenity. Justice William Brennan wrote:

All ideas having even the slightest redeeming [worthwhile] social importance—unorthodox ideas, controversial ideas, even ideas hateful to the prevailing climate of opinion—have the full protection of the guaranties [of the First Amendment].... But implicit [not expressly stated] in the history of the First Amendment is the rejection of obscenity as utterly without redeeming social importance.

Brennan then defined obscenity as the treatment of sex "in a manner appealing to prurient [immoral] interest."

To determine if something was obscene, Brennan said the Court would try to decide if an average person would consider the whole work to be immoral or offensive. If only parts of a work were offensive, this did not mean that the whole work could be called obscene.

Justices William O. Douglas and Hugo Black disagreed with the rest of the Court. Both justices believed in the people's absolute right to freedom of speech and press. This included obscenity. They said that the courts should not try to set up a moral code. Douglas wrote, "If the First Amendment guarantee of freedom of speech and press is to mean anything in this field, it must allow protests even against the moral code that the standard of the day sets for the community."

In 1964 the Court moved to a less strict definition of obscenity. This took place in the case of *Jacobellis* v. *Ohio*. The case involved an Ohio theater manager who was convicted of possessing and showing a film entitled *The Lovers*. The film had an explicit love scene. Justices Brennan and Goldberg wrote the Court's majority opinion. They said that in addition to appealing to a prurient, or immoral, interest, obscene material must be "utterly without redeeming social importance." This meant that works would no longer be judged as a whole, as the Court had said in the decision in the *Roth* case. Now if a work had *any* part that had some social value, then it was not obscene.

Brennan and Goldberg also said that obscenity could not be defined purely by local standards. Individual towns, cities, and states could not develop their own standards. Obscenity would now be determined by the same standard in all parts of the country. According to Brennan and Goldberg, "It is, after all, a national Constitution we are expounding," that is, explaining. This meant that freedom of the press could not mean one thing in one part of the country and another thing somewhere else. In Brennan and Goldberg's words:

> The Court has explicitly [clearly] refused to tolerate a result whereby "the constitutional limits of free expression in the Nation would vary with state lines." . . . We see even less justification for allowing such limits to vary with town or county lines.

Two years after the *Jacobellis* case, the Supreme Court issued its broadest protection of the people's right to obscene expression. In *A Book Named "John Cleland's Memoirs of a Woman of*

Pleasure" v. *Attorney-General of Massachusetts* (1966), the Court tried to decide if the novel *Fanny Hill* was obscene. The Court said something is obscene if it failed three tests. First, is the book "utterly without redeeming social value"? Second, does the book's "dominant [main] theme" appeal to an immoral interest? And finally, is "the material patently [plainly] offensive because it affronts [offends] contemporary community standards relating to the description or representation of sexual matters"?

The majority of the Court said that *Fanny Hill* passed these tests. They said the novel had value as a literary work. Justices Black and Douglas agreed that the book was not obscene. But again they argued strongly against any restrictions of a free press. According to Douglas, "Publications and utterances [sayings] were made immune [protected] from majoritarian control [control by the majority] by the First Amendment, applicable to the States by reason of the Fourteenth. No exceptions were made, not even for obscenity."

The *Fanny Hill* case did not settle the debate over obscenity. In the early 1970s, the Supreme Court began to place more limits on the people's right to obscene expression. This change was due to the addition of four new justices from 1969 to 1971: Chief Justice Warren Burger and Justices Harry Blackmun, Lewis Powell, Jr., and William Rehnquist. Republican President Richard Nixon appointed these justices for their conservative views. Each of them was less liberal about obscenity than those who served before them on the Court. Chief Justice Burger summed up their views when he wrote that "exploitation of obscene material demeans [lowers in dignity] the grand conception [idea] of the First Amendment and its high purposes in the historic struggle for freedom."

In 1973, the four Nixon justices and Justice Byron White voted to throw out the test used in the *Fanny Hill* case and set up a new one. This time it was the case of *Miller* v. *California.* According to Chief Justice Burger, obscenity no longer meant material that was "utterly without redeeming social value." From now on obscenity referred to any work that met three requirements. To be considered obscene, a work had to meet all three. One was that the material, when taken as a whole, did not have "serious literary, artistic, political, or scientific value."

The second requirement was that the "average person," using present-day "community standards" would find the work, taken as a whole, to appeal to immoral interest. The third requirement was that the work show sexual conduct that was not only clearly offensive but had been defined as such in state law. The Court's majority thus moved back to the idea of local standards for obscenity and away from Justices Brennan and Goldberg's ideas about a "national Constitution." The Court now agreed that individual communities could come up with their own definitions of obscenity. According to Burger:

> It is neither realistic nor constitutionally sound to read the First Amendment as requiring that the people of Maine or Mississippi accept public depiction [showing] of conduct found tolerable in Las Vegas or New York City. People in different States vary in their tastes and attitudes, and this diversity is not to be strangled by the absolutism of imposed uniformity.

Again Justice Douglas led the charge against this opinion. The idea that the First Amendment protected only "serious" forms of speech and press concerned Douglas. In his view, the government could possibly stop publication of or censor anything it wanted to by claiming it was not "serious." Justice Brennan echoed this idea. He said that "the protections of the First Amendment have never been thought limited to expressions of serious literary or political value."

The decision in the *Miller* case did not give communities the freedom to forbid anything that they considered to be obscene. In 1974 the Court ruled that a Georgia town could not forbid the showing of the film *Carnal Knowledge* because it considered the film to be obscene. Justice Rehnquist wrote that the movie was not obscene because it did not "depict sexual conduct in a patently [clearly] offensive way." According to Rehnquist, though the movie contained nudity, "nudity alone is not enough to make material legally obscene."

In 1982 the Court ruled that states could forbid the production and distribution of child pornography (pornography is material with a strong sexual content). According to the Court, this was still the case even if the material could not be considered legally obscene. Justice White wrote that child pornography was closely related to child abuse and caused mental harm to the children involved. Therefore, all the justices agreed that the necessity of protecting children outweighed any First Amendment concerns.

Obscenity in Art and Music

Controversy over obscenity in art erupted in 1989. The turmoil began when Senator Jesse Helms and others criticized the National Endowment for the Arts (NEA). The NEA is a government agency that provides financial grants to artists and museums.

Helms accused the NEA of supporting obscene art and proposed that Congress cut back its funding of the agency. He said the NEA had contributed to artists whose artwork were obscene or antireligious or had homosexual content. The NEA reacted by canceling grants for several controversial artists. It did this in the hope of stopping Congress from cutting off its funds or placing severe limits on the type of art it could support.

Many artists and supporters of civil liberties protested these moves. They said that the government was censoring the arts, or forbidding the display or publication of any material that it does not approve.

Others argued that restricting NEA funds for certain types of art was not censorship. They claimed artists were still free to create what they wished. They merely stated that the government does not have to give tax money to art it does not approve. Also, artists could always turn down NEA grants. That way, they would be sure of not being censored.

Senator Jesse Helms of North Carolina led the fight against government funding for art that he and many other Americans regarded as obscene.

Part of the NEA controversy centered on the work of photographer Robert Mapplethorpe. Senator Helms and other conservatives had criticized Mapplethorpe's photographs for their homosexual content. As a result, a Washington, D.C., museum canceled a showing of Mapplethorpe's work for fear of losing its NEA funds. Then, in Cincinnati, Ohio, a local museum director was charged with breaking a local antiobscenity law when he showed Mapplethorpe's work. The museum director was found not guilty of the obscenity charges.

The outcry over obscenity in the arts came as many people also voiced concern about lyrics in rock and rap music. In the late 1980s some religious and parents' groups put pressure on Congress and

Protesters in Cincinnati demand an end to art exhibits that they believe are obscene. In 1990, a local court ruled that photographs by Robert Mapplethorpe in an exhibit were not obscene.

state lawmakers to pass laws requiring record companies to place warning labels on records with lyrics the groups found offensive. These groups claimed the labels would help parents choose what they wanted their children to hear. Others, especially in the music industry, argued that the labels were censorship.

One well-known case of obscenity in music involved the rap group 2 Live Crew. In 1990, a federal district judge in Florida ruled that the group's songs were obscene. Two days after the decision, police arrested a Florida record store owner for selling a copy of the group's album "As Nasty as They Wanna Be." A few days later, police arrested three of the 2 Live Crew's members at one of their concerts.

The 2 Live Crew controversy divided people. Some claimed that their songs were obscene and insulting to women. Others argued that the government had no right to decide what forms of art were or were not obscene. They believed that people should be free to listen and see what they wished. Later in 1990, a Fort Lauderdale jury found the members of the 2 Live Crew not guilty of obscenity.

At the center of the debate over obscenity are two important rights—the rights of individual citizens and the rights of communities. The first is the right of people to decide for themselves what they can see, read, or think. It is this right that is found in the First Amendment. The other is the right of a community to set certain rules and standards of behavior for everyone to live by. The democratic idea of majority rule is based upon this right.

Which of these rights is more important? No one can say for sure. Ideas of how best to balance these two rights vary from person to person, from community to community, and from era to era. Of one thing we can be sure. More questions and debates about obscenity lie ahead.

Freedom of Assembly

"[P]eaceable assembly for lawful discussion cannot be made a crime."
CHIEF JUSTICE CHARLES EVANS HUGHES, in *DeJonge* v. *Oregon* (1937)

The United States has been called a nation of joiners. Across the country there are thousands, perhaps even hundreds of thousands, of political and civic groups. The First Amendment protects the people's right to join these groups. The final section of the First Amendment says that Congress shall make no law abridging "the right of the people peaceably to assemble, and to petition the government for a redress of grievances."

This means that people have a right to hold meetings and form and join associations to try to influence the government. The founders of the country knew that without this freedom, the other rights in the First Amendment would be of little value. They knew that individual citizens have limited power to influence government. But they knew that if individual citizens came together in associations and groups, then they can do many things.

People exercise this right in many ways. Some groups are small. Such a group might be ten or twelve neighbors who hold a public meeting to ask that a stop sign be placed at a dangerous street

---

Daisy Bates, head of the Arkansas NAACP, in a courtroom in 1958. Her eventual court victory strengthened freedom of association rights linked to the First Amendment.

crossing. Other groups are larger. An example might be a citizens' group that lobbies the state legislature to clean up a toxic waste dump. Other groups, like political parties, span the nation. It is their aim to seek to control the government, not just to influence it.

Like most other rights, freedom of assembly and association has not always been protected. This freedom has often been denied to unpopular groups. Political radicals, labor unions, and civil rights groups have all seen this liberty denied to them at some point in our nation's history.

The Supreme Court began to support the people's right to political association in 1937. The case involved Dirk DeJonge, a Communist party member from Portland, Oregon. The police arrested DeJonge when he spoke at a meeting. They claimed the gathering was an illegal meeting of the Communist party. A jury agreed with the police and sentenced DeJonge to jail.

DeJonge appealed his case to the U.S. Supreme Court. He held that his arrest and conviction violated the First Amendment's protection of a person's right to free assembly. He said that the meeting he spoke at was not a gathering of the Communist party. Instead, he claimed that the meeting was to discuss police brutality during a recent strike and the poor conditions in the county jail.

All of the justices agreed with DeJonge. They said that the Fourteenth Amendment meant that states could not deny the people's right to peaceful assembly and political association. The Court also stated that the meeting was a peaceful public assembly protected by the First Amendment. Chief Justice Charles Evans Hughes wrote:

[P]eacable assembly for lawful discussion cannot be made a crime. The holding of meetings for peaceable political action cannot be proscribed. These who assist in the conduct of such meetings cannot be branded as criminals on that score.

Chief Justice Hughes's strong argument for freedom of assembly and association was not enough to withstand the cold war and the McCarthy era. In the late 1940s and early 1950s, fear of communism led the government to limit the people's right to freedom of assembly and association. Congress passed laws forbidding people from joining suspected Communist organizations. Committees in Congress forced witnesses to tell of their past or present membership in groups linked to the Communist party. Those who had been members of these groups found themselves "blacklisted." Persons on the "blacklists" soon lost their jobs. Others found that no one would hire them. Many famous playwrights, screenwriters, directors, and actors found themselves on the "blacklists."

The Supreme Court agreed with many of the limits on the people's right to freedom of assembly and association. In 1952 six justices voted to uphold a New York law that allowed school boards to fire teachers who were or had been members of subversive organizations. A subversive organization is one that wants to overthrow the government or undo it. Justice Sherman Minton wrote in the Court's opinion:

> That the school authorities have the right and the duty to screen the officials, teachers and employees as to their fitness to maintain the integrity of the schools as part of ordered society, cannot be doubted. One's associates, past and present, as well as one's conduct, may properly be considered in determining fitness and loyalty. From time immemorial, [before memory, records, or tradition], one's reputation has been determined in part by the company he keeps.

Three justices disagreed with the Court's decision. One of them, Justice William O. Douglas, said that the New York law "proceeds on a principle repugnant [hateful] to our society—guilt by association." He said the law created a situation where "Youthful indiscretions [mistakes], mistaken causes, misguided enthusiasms—all long forgotten—become the ghosts of a harrowing [disturbing] present." Douglas added that teachers should be judged by their skill in the classroom, not by the political groups they belong to.

In 1961 the Court voted to uphold the McCarran Act (1950).

This law required the Communist party and related groups to register with the government. They also had to provide lists of their members. Justice Felix Frankfurter and four other justices ruled that the act did not violate freedom of assembly and association. In the words of Frankfurter:

> Where the mask of anonymity [being secret] which an organization's members wear serves the double purpose of protecting them from popular prejudice and of enabling them to cover over a foreign-directed conspiracy, infiltrate [make one's way into] other groups, and enlist the support of persons who would not if the truth were revealed, lend their support . . . it would be a distortion of the First Amendment to hold that it prohibits Congress from removing the mask.

Four justices said that they believed the McCarran Act violated the First Amendment. Justice Hugo Black warned that this act placed the nation in danger of tyranny. He wrote:

> The first banning of an association because it advocates hated ideas . . . marks a fateful moment in the history of a free country. That moment seems to have arrived for this country. . . . When the practice of outlawing parties and various public groups begins, no one can say where it will end. In most countries such a practice once begun ends with a one-party government.

In this case the Supreme Court allowed the government to limit Communists' right of association. The Court refused, however, to allow governments to limit the right of association of members of all political groups. In two cases, the Court ruled that states and local governments could not force civil rights organizations to register and turn over their membership lists.

The first case began in Montgomery, Alabama, on December 1, 1955. Montgomery and most other places in the South in 1955 still practiced segregation. This meant blacks and whites could not share the same facilities such as restaurants, restrooms, and schools. They could ride the same buses, but African Americans were forced to sit in the back. Equality did not exist.

On that day Rosa Parks, an African-American woman, was riding home on the bus. The bus began to fill with white riders. The driver called for the black riders to move to the back of the bus and give up their seats to the whites. As the other blacks began to move, Parks thought for a moment. She knew she would be arrested if she kept her seat. She was tired from work. But she also thought it was wrong for her to give up her seat to a white man. Rosa Parks stayed where she was.

Parks's decision was the spark that set off the civil rights movement. Her arrest led to a boycott of the Montgomery buses. African Americans refused to ride the buses and chose to walk or share car rides instead. The boycott was long and difficult, but it succeeded. The legal battles led all the way up to the Supreme Court. Segregation on public transportation in Alabama was declared illegal. In December 1956, Montgomery's bus segregation laws were officially ended. Montgomery allowed the races to sit together on buses. This success showed the way for others who would challenge racism and segregation.

Many persons and groups were important to the success of the boycott. One of the groups that helped was the Alabama Chapter of the National Association for the Advancement of Colored People (NAACP). Rosa Parks had been an active NAACP member long before her arrest. Because of the NAACP's role in the boycott, the state of Alabama tried to put it out of business.

In 1956 Alabama's attorney general found a little known state law. That law required out-of-state organizations, like the NAACP, to register with the state and turn over their membership lists. Because the NAACP had not registered he convinced an Alabama judge to order them to stop all activities in Alabama.

In time the NAACP did register with the state, but refused to turn over its membership lists. The NAACP's leaders knew that if they gave up the names, their members would become victims of

Rosa Parks, an active NAACP member, sitting in the front of a Montgomery, Alabama, bus. The Supreme Court had just ruled that a Montgomery law requiring segregated buses was unconstitutional.

harassment and violence. The judge refused to accept their argument. He fined the NAACP $100,000.

The NAACP took its case to the U.S. Supreme Court. In 1958 all the justices of the Supreme Court ruled that Alabama's actions were illegal. It said that freedom of association was crucial to the First Amendment. It also said that the forced naming of the NAACP's members violated this freedom. Justice John Marshall Harlan wrote:

Effective advocacy of both public and private points of view, particularly controversial ones, is undeniably enhanced [improved] by group association. . . . The Court has recognized the vital relationship between freedom to associate and privacy in one's associations. Inviolability [safety] of privacy in group association may in many circumstances be indispensable [absolutely necessary] to preservation of freedom of association, particularly where the group espouses [voices] dissident beliefs.

Before the Supreme Court could speak on this issue, Little Rock, Arkansas, passed a law similar to Alabama's. Little Rock's law was passed in October 1957. This was one month after the city erupted into conflict as African Americans were integrated into white schools.

In an attempt to help win reelection, Arkansas's governor, Orval Faubus, stirred up violent protests by whites against the black students. Faubus then called in the Arkansas National Guard to prevent bloodshed. He did not use the guards to stop the white mobs. Instead, he used it to stop the black students from entering school.

The next day Elizabeth Eckford, a fifteen-year-old black student, tried to enter Little Rock's Central High School. National Guardsmen armed with rifles and bayonets blocked her way. Then a crowd of angry whites surrounded her. They shouted, "Get her!" "Lynch her!" "Get a rope and drag her over to this tree!" Eventually a friendly white woman helped Elizabeth escape from the mob.

The events in Little Rock shocked the nation. Millions of people saw Elizabeth's brave stand on their televisions. President Dwight Eisenhower sent in the U.S. Army. The army stopped the violence and allowed the African-American students to enter school.

After failing to stop integration of the schools, the white leaders of Little Rock decided to punish the local NAACP. The NAACP had played an important role in getting Little Rock's schools integrated. Daisy Bates, the head of the Arkansas NAACP, had become a national celebrity during the crisis.

Encouraged by Arkansas's attorney general, Little Rock's city council passed a law requiring the NAACP to submit the names of its members. When Bates and the Reverend J. C. Crenchaw, the president of the Little Rock NAACP, refused to hand over the names, the city council voted to have them arrested. Though she was only fined $100 and despite threats against her, Bates decided to appeal her case.

Bates's case reached the U.S. Supreme Court in 1960. As in the *Alabama* case, the Court voted as a body that the Little Rock law violated freedom of association. Justice Potter Stewart wrote the Court's opinion. He relied heavily upon Justice Harlan's previous opinion in the *Alabama* case. He said that the threats against Bates showed what could happen when people did not have a right to privacy in their associations.

The tensions of the cold war began to lessen in the 1960s. At this time the Supreme Court began to reconsider some of its opinions. Throughout the decade, the Court upheld the freedom of association for Communists. The high point of this trend came in 1967. That year the Court ruled that the freedom of association even allowed Communists to work in defense plants as long as national security was not hurt.

The case involved a Communist party member named Robel. Robel was a worker in a Seattle shipyard. The shipyard did defense-related work. When it became known that Robel was a Communist, he was fired and charged with violating the McCarran Act (1950). One part of the McCarran Act made it illegal for Communists to work in jobs related to national defense. Working in a shipyard was such a job.

Robel appealed his case to the U.S. Supreme Court. The Court voted 6 to 2 that this section of the McCarran Act was unconstitutional. Though Robel was a Communist, the Court did not believe he posed a threat to national security in his job. Since the law forced Robel to choose between his job and his political group, the Court ruled that it was unconstitutional. According to Chief Justice Earl Warren, the McCarran Act

> put appellate [Robel] to the choice of surrendering his organizational affiliation, regardless of whether his membership threatened

the security of a defense facility or giving up his job. . . . The statute [law] quite literally establishes guilt by association alone. . . . The inhibiting effect of the exercise of First Amendment rights is clear.

Justices Byron White and John Marshall Harlan disagreed with the rest of the Court. They recognized that some Communists could safely hold defense-related jobs. But, they added, there was no way to know which Communists were safe and which were not. They therefore believed that it was legal for Congress to pass a law forbidding the hiring of Communists for defense jobs. In their view the requirements of national security outweighed an individual citizen's right to freedom of association.

Since the time of the decision in the *Robel* case, the Court has kept up its protection of the people's right to freedom of association and assembly. This means that people can freely join the political groups that they wish, even if those groups are unpopular. It also allows people to be judged on their own merits. They cannot be found guilty because of the company they keep.

CHAPTER 13

Conclusion

"Congress shall make no law respecting an establishment of religion, or prohibiting the free exercise thereof; or abridging the freedom of speech, or of the press; or the right of the people peaceably to assemble, and to petition the Government for a redress of grievances."

THE FIRST AMENDMENT TO THE UNITED STATES CONSTITUTION

At the beginning of this book you read that the First Amendment was like a star that has helped guide our nation on its journey through history. This journey has been long and marked by many important events. It has taken our nation through triumphs and tragedies: the Revolution, the founding of the nation, the Civil War, World Wars I and II, the civil rights movement, and the war in Vietnam among them.

Throughout this journey there have been many debates over the meaning of the First Amendment. Some have argued that the rights protected by the First Amendment are absolute. This means they cannot be violated for any reason. Others have argued that those rights must be balanced with other important goals. Some of these goals are order, majority rule, and national security.

But these debates have not kept the rights protected by the First Amendment from growing stronger. As a nation we have become more tolerant of different ideas and beliefs. We hold more deeply the belief that the freedom to choose and express our beliefs is one of our nation's greatest strengths.

The Supreme Court Building in Washington, D.C., was designed by Cass Gilbert and completed in 1935.

But our freedoms have not grown stronger because of U.S. Supreme Court justices or other powerful people. Our freedoms have become stronger because ordinary people have had the courage to stand up for their rights. By fighting for their freedoms Eugene Debs, Ishmael Jaffree, John Scopes, Susan Epperson, Dan Seeger, Jay Near, Elmer Gertz, Dirk DeJonge, Rosa Parks, and many others helped to make freedom more secure for the rest of us. They had little money or power. What they did have was courage and a belief in justice.

Many of those who fought for their First Amendment rights were students. William and Lillian Gobitis, Marie Barnette, Yetta Stromberg, Mary Beth Tinker, Lauren Boyd, Gina Gambino, and others all fought for freedom when many adults would not.

The stories in this book show us that it is the job of all Americans, young and old alike, to keep the First Amendment strong. This means being ready to fight to protect and strengthen our rights. But it also means rejecting fear and intolerance that might cause us to take freedom from others. If we do our job, then the First Amendment will continue to guide our nation in the future.

$\mathscr{I}$MPORTANT $\mathscr{D}$ATES

1735   Trial of John Peter Zenger helps to establish freedom of the press in the American colonies.

1775   American Revolution begins.

1776   Declaration of Independence is signed.

1776   Virginia Constitution and Declaration of Rights are adopted.

1783   Revolutionary War ends.

1787   Constitutional Convention writes U.S. Constitution.

1788   U.S. Constitution is ratified by most states.

1789   New federal government set up by the U.S. Constitution begins its work.

1789   Madison proposes and Congress passes the Bill of Rights.

1791   Bill of Rights is ratified by the states.

1798   Alien and Sedition Acts are passed.

1833   U.S. Supreme Court decides the case of *Barron* v. *Baltimore*. Says that the Bill of Rights does not apply to the states.

1861   Civil War begins.

1865   Civil War ends.

1868   Fourteenth Amendment is ratified by the states. States cannot deny the "privileges or immunities" of its citizens or take away their "life, liberty, or property, without due process of law."

1917   The United States enters World War I.

1917   Russian Revolution takes place, and the "Red Scare" begins.

1919   U.S. Supreme Court decides the *Schenck, Debs*, and *Abrams* cases. Justice Oliver Wendell Holmes develops a doctrine of "clear and present danger."

1925   U.S. Supreme Court rules in *Gitlow* v. *New York* that freedom of speech is protected from state laws by the Fourteenth Amendment.

1925   *Scopes* trial in Dayton, Tennessee, debates evolution versus creationism.

1931   U.S. Supreme Court declares in *Near* v. *Minnesota* that freedom of the press is protected from state laws by the Fourteenth Amendment.

1931   U.S. Supreme Court begins to protect the people's right to freedom of speech in *Stromberg* v. *California*.

1935   William and Lillian Gobitis refuse to salute the flag.

1937   U.S. Supreme Court rules in *DeJonge* v. *Oregon* that freedom of association and assembly is protected from state laws by the Fourteenth Amendment.

1939   World War II begins in Europe.

1940   U.S. Supreme Court declares in *Cantwell* v. *Connecticut* that the people's right to free exercise of religion is protected from state laws by the Fourteenth Amendment.

1940   U.S. Supreme Court rules flag salute laws are constitutional in the *Gobitis* case.

1941   United States enters World War II.

1942 Marie Barnette refuses to salute the flag.

1942 U.S. Supreme Court says that the First Amendment does not protect the people's right to use "fighting words" in *Chaplinsky* v. *New Hampshire.*

1943 U.S. Supreme Court rules that flag salute laws are unconstitutional in the *Barnette* case.

1945 World War II ends; the cold war begins.

1947 Leaders of the American Communist party are arrested.

1947 U.S. Supreme Court rules in *Everson* v. *Board of Education* that the Fourteenth Amendment protects against the establishment of religion by the states.

1950 Korean War begins.

1951 U.S. Supreme Court restricts freedom of speech for Communists in *Dennis et al.* v. *United States.*

1953 Korean War ends.

1953 Earl Warren appointed chief justice of the United States.

1954 U.S. Supreme Court declares school segregation unconstitutional.

1955 Civil rights movement begins with Montgomery bus boycott.

1957 Little Rock school desegregation crisis.

1957 U.S. Supreme Court in *Yates* v. *United States* makes it harder to deny the people their right to freedom of speech.

1957 U.S. Supreme Court decides first obscenity case, *Roth* v. *United States.*

1957 Dan Seeger declares his opposition to the military draft.

1958 U.S. Supreme Court strikes down Alabama's ban on the National Association for the Advancement of Colored People (NAACP).

1960 Black students begin sit-ins at segregated lunch counters.

1960 U.S. Supreme Court strikes down Little Rock's anti-NAACP law.

1961 U.S. Supreme Court upholds the McCarran Act (1950), saying that freedom of association does not extend to Communists.

1961 U.S. Supreme Court says sit-ins are a constitutional form of symbolic speech.

1961 U.S. Supreme Court strikes down "blue laws."

1962 U.S. Supreme Court strikes down state-sponsored school prayer in *Engel* v. *Vitale.*

1964 U.S. Supreme Court says that the people's right to freedom of the press protects the media from most libel cases in *New York Times* v. *Sullivan.*

1964 Large U.S. military involvement in Vietnam War begins.

1964 U.S. Supreme Court expands protection of the people's right to freedom of expression, in *Jacobellis* v. *Ohio*, an obscenity case.

1965 U.S. Supreme Court rules that states cannot forbid the teaching of evolution in *Epperson* v. *Arkansas.*

1965 U.S. Supreme Court rules that the draft violates Dan Seeger's right to free exercise of religion.

1965 Mary Beth Tinker wears a black armband to school to protest the Vietnam War.

1966 Sidney Street burns the American flag to protest the shooting of James Meredith.

1967 U.S. Supreme Court in the *Robel* case rules that the McCarran Act (1950) violates the people's right to freedom of assembly and association.

1969 U.S. Supreme Court rules in *Brandenburg* v. *Ohio* that only the most dangerous forms of speech can be forbidden by law.

1969 U.S. Supreme Court says that the First Amendment protects Mary Beth Tinker's right to wear a black armband to school.

1970 United States invades Cambodia during the Vietnam War.

1971 *Pentagon Papers* case.

1973 U.S. Supreme Court restricts the people's right to freedom of expression in *Miller* v. *California*, an obscenity case.

1973 U.S. military involvement in Vietnam War ends.

1977 American Nazis attempt to march in Skokie, Illinois.

1979 U.S. Supreme Court says in *Herbert* v. *Lando* that reporters must reveal their "state of mind" in libel cases.

1984 Gregory Lee Johnson burns the U.S. flag at the Republican National Convention in Dallas, Texas.

1987 U.S. Supreme Court strikes down Louisiana law requiring equal time for the teaching of creationism and evolution in its schools.

1988 U.S. Supreme Court rules that schools can censor student newspapers in the *Hazelwood High School* case.

1989 U.S. Supreme Court rules in *Texas* v. *Johnson* that the First Amendment protects a person's right to burn the U.S. flag as a symbolic action.

1989 U.S. Congress passes a law making flag burning illegal.

1989 Controversy over federal funding of obscene art begins.

1990 Controversy over obscene music lyrics grows with arrest and trial of rap group 2 Live Crew.

1990 U.S. Supreme Court says that the federal law against flag burning is unconstitutional.

1990 Constitutional amendment banning flag burning fails to pass U.S. Congress.

1990 U.S. Supreme Court tries to balance freedom of the press with the right to a fair trial in the *CNN/Noriega* case.

amendment   A change in the Constitution.

appeal   To refer a case to a higher court to review the decision of a lower court.

bail   Money paid by the accused to gain his or her release in the period before trial to make sure he or she will show up for the trial. If the accused does not, he or she loses the money.

bill of attainder   A law pronouncing a person guilty of a serious crime without a trial.

blue laws   Laws regulating work and entertainment activities on Sundays.

concurring opinion   A separate opinion delivered by one or more judges that agrees with the majority opinion's decision but offers different reasons for reaching that decision.

conscientious objector   One who because of religious or ethical training and belief is opposed to taking part in war.

dissenting opinion   An opinion by one or more of a court's judges that disagrees with a majority opinion.

double jeopardy   The putting of a person on trial for a crime for which he or she has already been put on trial.

executive branch   The branch or part of the government that carries the laws into effect and makes sure they are obeyed.

ex post facto **laws**   Laws that make illegal those actions that took place before the passage of the law.

federalism   The relationships between the states and the federal government, each having certain special powers and sharing others.

fighting words   Speech not protected by the Constitution as free speech if it is by its very wording likely to bring about violent reaction from the audience.

immunity   Freedom from penalties and duties.

incorporation   The process of making the rights in the Bill of Rights apply to the states so that people are guaranteed to be safeguarded against state actions that might violate their rights. The Fourteenth Amendment's due process clause is used as the basis for this process.

indictment   A grand jury's written accusation naming the person charged with a crime and charging that person with the crime.

judicial branch   The part or branch of the government that interprets the laws and settles disputes under the law.

judicial review   The power of the courts to review the decisions of other parts or levels of the government. Courts may review the decisions of lower courts and come to a different decision.

legislative branch   The part or branch of the government that makes the laws.

majority opinion   The statement of the decision of a court in which the majority of its members join.

prior restraint   Any system that gives public officials the power to deny freedom of speech or freedom of the press in advance of the actual expression.

ratification   Approval of the amendment by three-fourths of state legislatures or conventions (after the amendment has been officially proposed by two-thirds of each house of Congress or proposed by a convention called by two-thirds of the states).

separation of powers   The division of the government into three parts or branches—the legislative, the executive, and the judicial.

symbolic speech   A person's conduct that expresses thoughts or opinions about a subject and that may or may not be protected by the First Amendment.

$\mathcal{S}$UGGESTED $\mathcal{R}$EADING

Abraham, Henry J. *Freedom and the Court: Civil Rights and Liberties in the United States*. New York: Oxford University Press, 1988.

*Arbetman, Lee, McMahon, Edward, and O'Brien, Edward. *Street Law: A Course in Practical Law,* 3rd ed. St. Paul, Minn.: West Publishing, 1980.

*Arbetman, Lee, and Richard Poe. *Great Trials in American History: Civil War to the Present*. St. Paul, Minn.: West Publishing, 1984.

*American Political Science Association and American Historical Association, ed. *This Constitution: From Ratification to the Bill of Rights*. Washington, D.C.: Congressional Quarterly, 1988.

The Bill of Rights and Beyond: A Resource Guide. The Commission on the Bicentennial of the United States Constitution, 1990.

*Brant, Irving. *The Bill of Rights: Its Origins and Meaning*. Indianapolis: Bobbs-Merrill, 1965.

*Cox, Archibald. *The Court and the Constitution*. Boston: Houghton Mifflin, 1987.

*Friendly, Fred. *Minnesota Rag*. New York: Vintage Books, 1981.

*Hentoff, Nat. *The First Freedom: The Tumultuous History of Free Speech in America*. New York: Delacorte, 1980.

*Irons, Peter. *The Courage of Their Convictions: Sixteen Americans Who Fought Their Way to the Supreme Court*. New York: Penguin Books, 1990.

Kalven, Harry, Jr. *A Worthy Tradition: Freedom of Speech in America*. New York: Harper and Row, 1988.

Larson, Edward J. *Trial and Error: The American Controversy Over Creation and Evolution*. New York: Oxford University Press, 1985.

Levy, Leonard W. *Freedom of Speech and Press in Early American History: Legacy of Suppression*. New York: Harper and Row, 1963.

Levy, Leonard W., Kenneth L. Karst, and Dennis J. Mahoney. *Encyclopedia of the American Constitution*. New York: Macmillan, 1986.

Meiklejohn, Alexander. *Political Freedom: The Constitutional Powers of the People*. New York: Oxford University Press, 1965.

Morgan, Richard E. *The Supreme Court and Religion*. New York: Free Press, 1972.

*Petracca, Mark P. "What Every Student Should Know About the Bill of Rights." *The Political Science Teacher* 3 (Spring 1990): pp. 10–12.

Pfeffer, Leo. *Religious Freedom*. Skokie, Ill.: National Textbook Co., 1977.

Rutland, Robert. *The Birth of the Bill of Rights, 1776–1791*. Chapel Hill: University of North Carolina Press, 1955.

Smith, Edward Conrad, and Harold J. Spaeth, ed. *The Constitution of the United States*. New York: Barnes and Noble, 1987.

Smith, Page. *The Constitution: A Documentary and Narrative History.* New York: Morrow, 1978.

*Starr, Isidore. *The Idea of Liberty: First Amendment Freedoms.* St. Paul, Minn.: West Publishing, 1978.

*Stevens, Leonard A. *Salute! The Case of the Bible vs. the Flag. Great Constitutional Issues: The First Amendment.* New York: Coward, McCann, and Geoghegan, 1973.

Witt, Elder. *The Supreme Court and Individual Rights.* Washington, D.C.: Congressional Quarterly, 1988.

*Readers of *The First Amendment* by Philip A. Klinkner will find these books particularly readable.

$\mathscr{S}$OURCES

Abraham, Henry J. *Freedom and the Court: Civil Rights and Liberties in the United States.* 5th ed. New York: Oxford University Press, 1988.

American Political Science Association and the American Historical Association, ed. *This Constitution: From Ratification to the Bill of Rights.* Washington, D.C.: Congressional Quarterly, 1988.

Brant, Irving. *The Bill of Rights: Its Origins and Meaning.* Indianapolis: Bobbs-Merrill, 1965.

Brant, Irving. *James Madison: Father of the Constitution, 1787–1800.* Indianapolis: Bobbs-Merrill, 1950.

Cox, Archibald. *The Court and the Constitution.* Boston: Houghton Mifflin, 1987.

Emerson, Thomas I. *Toward a General Theory of the First Amendment.* New York: Random House, 1963.

Friendly, Fred. *Minnesota Rag.* New York: Vintage Books, 1981.

Gunther, Gerald. *Constitutional Law,* 11th ed. Mineola, New York: Foundation Press, 1985.

Hamlin, David. *The Nazi/Skokie Conflict: A Civil Liberties Battle.* Boston: Beacon Press, 1980.

Harris, Richard. *Freedom Spent: Tales of Tyranny in America.* Boston: Little, Brown, 1974.

Hentoff, Nat. *The First Freedom: The Tumultuous History of Free Speech in America.* New York: Delacorte, 1980.

Irons, Peter. *The Courage of Their Convictions: Sixteen Americans Who Fought Their Way to the Supreme Court.* New York: Penguin Books, 1990.

Kalven, Harry, Jr. *A Worthy Tradition: Freedom of Speech in America.* New York: Harper and Row, 1988.

Larson, Edward J. *Trial and Error: The American Controversy Over Creation and Evolution.* New York: Oxford University Press, 1985.

Levy, Leonard W. *Freedom of Speech and Press in Early American History: Legacy of Suppression.* New York: Harper and Row, 1963.

Levy, Leonard W., Kenneth L. Karst, and Dennis J. Mahoney. *Encyclopedia of the American Constitution.* New York: Macmillan, 1986.

McBrien, Richard P. *Caesar's Coin: Religion and Politics in America.* New York: Macmillan, 1987.

Meiklejohn, Alexander. *Political Freedom: The Constitutional Powers of the People.* New York: Oxford University Press, 1965.

Morgan, Richard E. *The Supreme Court and Religion.* New York: Free Press, 1972.

Petracca, Mark P. "What Every Student Should Know About the Bill of Rights." *The Political Science Teacher* 3 (Spring 1990): pp. 10–12.

Pfeffer, Leo. *Religious Freedom.* Skokie, Ill.: National Textbook Co., 1977.

Pole, J. R., ed. *The American Constitution: For and Against: The Federalist and Anti-Federalist Papers.* New York: Hill and Wang, 1987.

Rutland, Robert. *The Birth of the Bill of Rights, 1776–1791.* Chapel Hill: University of North Carolina Press, 1955.

Schwartz, Bernard. *The Great Rights of Mankind: A History of the American Bill of Rights.* New York: Oxford University Press, 1977.

Schwartz, Bernard. *Super Chief: Earl Warren and His Supreme Court—A Judicial Biography.* New York: New York University Press, 1983.

Smith, Edward Conrad, and Harold J. Spaeth, ed. *The Constitution of the United States.* New York: Barnes and Noble, 1987.

Smith, Page. *The Constitution: A Documentary and Narrative History.* New York: Morrow, 1978.

Stevens, Leonard A. *Salute! The Case of the Bible vs. the Flag. Great Constitutional Issues: The First Amendment.* New York: Coward, McCann, and Geoghegan, 1973.

Witt, Elder. *The Supreme Court and Individual Rights.* Washington D.C.: Congressional Quarterly, 1988.

$\mathscr{I}$ NDEX OF $\mathscr{C}$ ASES

$\mathscr{I}$NDEX

Philip Klinkner graduated from Lake Forest College in 1985 and is now finishing his Ph.D. in political science at Yale University. He is currently a Governmental Studies Fellow at the Brookings Institution in Washington, D.C. Klinkner is also the author of *The Ninth Amendment* volume in *The American Heritage History of the Bill of Rights*.

Warren E. Burger was Chief Justice of the United States from 1969 to 1986. Since 1985 he has served as chairman of the Commission on the Bicentennial of the United States Constitution. He is also chancellor of the College of William and Mary, Williamsburg, Virginia; chancellor emeritus of the Smithsonian Institution; and a life trustee of the National Geographic Society. Prior to his appointment to the Supreme Court, Chief Justice Burger was Assistant Attorney General of the United States (Civil Division) and judge of the United States Court of Appeals, District of Columbia Circuit.

Photograph Credits

Cover: © by J.L. Atlan/Sygma; 2–3: Independence Hall National Park; 10: © Dean Brown/Omni-Photo Communications; 10 (inset): Colonial Williamsburg; 11 (top): © Brad Markel/Gamma-Liaison; 11 (bottom): © Dean Brown/Omni-Photo Communications; 12: Michael Stucky/Comstock; 14: Colonial Williamsburg; 16: "Raising the Liberty Pole" by John McRae/Kennedy Galleries; 18–19: Independence Hall National Park; 28: Wally McNamee/Woodfin Camp & Associates, Inc.; 31: Courtesy of Lillian Gobitis Klose; 34 and 40: UPI/Bettmann Newsphotos; 42 and 46: Culver Pictures, Inc.; 48: Massachusetts Historical Society; 52: The Granger Collection; 56 and 58: Culver Pictures, Inc.; 62 and 66: UPI/Bettmann Newsphotos; 68: Bettmann Archive; 71: UPI/Bettmann Newsphotos; 76: © Bernard Gotfryd/Woodfin Camp & Associates, Inc.; 80, 83, and 87: UPI/Bettmann Newsphotos; 90: © Chuck O'Rear/Woodfin Camp & Associates, Inc.; 97: UPI/Bettmann Newsphotos; 100: Bettmann Archive; 102: UPI/Bettmann Newsphotos; 104: Brigham Young University; 108: UPI/Bettmann Newsphotos; 111: Karolik Collection/Museum of Fine Arts, Boston; 114: TSW Click Chicago/Charles Gupton; 119, 124, 130, and 133: UPI/Bettmann Newsphotos; 136: Courtesy of Elmer Gertz; 140: © Jacques Chenet/Woodfin Camp & Associates, Inc.; 147: © John Ficara/Woodfin Camp & Associates, Inc.; 148, 150, and 156: UPI/Bettmann Newsphotos, Inc.; 160: Imagefinders, Inc.